OFF THE BEATEN TRACK

Off the Beaten Track

J.H.B. PEEL

First published in Great Britain 1984

ISBN 0 7090 1547 X

Robert Hale Limited.
Clerkenwell House, Clerkenwell Green
London EC1R 0HT

Photoset by P.R.G. Graphics Ltd.,
Printed in Great Britain by
Photobooks (Bristol) Ltd, Barton Manor, St Philips, Bristol.
Bound by WBC Bookbinders Ltd.

Contents

1	Doone Land: Devon and Somerset	7
2	Off the Beaten Track: Buckinghamshire	15
3	Ultima Thule: Caithness and Sutherland	21
4	The Spirit of Delight: Sussex	31
5	A Glimpse of Paradise: Brecknockshire	40
6	The Old Straight Road: Gloucestershire and Wiltshire	46
7	Gathering of the Clans: Perthshire and Aberdeenshire	55
8	After the Storm: Dorset	64
9	A West-of-Wessex Girl: Cornwall	72
10	Sacred Mountains: Pembrokeshire	82
11	A Shepherd's Life: Hampshire	89
12	Good Taste: Rutland	99
13	An Incomparable Young Man: Oxford-shire	107
14	Away from it All: Shropshire	119
15	The Happiest Man on Earth: Berkshire	123
16	A Glittering Prospect: Carmarthenshire	131
17	The Deserted Village: Northumberland	139
18	A Slough of Despond: Perthshire	145
19	Up the Creek: Cornwall	149
20	The Modern Middle Ages: Nottinghamshire	154
21	No Man's Land: Roxburghshire	159

A Green Road: Westmorland 170
Ichabod: Berkshire and Wiltshire 172

Other books by J.H.B. Peel include:

POETRY
Light and Shade
Places and People

ESSAYS
Country Talk
More Country Talk
New Country Talk
Country Talk Again
Country Talk Continued
Latest Country Talk
Another Country Talk

TRAVEL
Portrait of the Thames
Portrait of the Severn
Portrait of Exmoor
Along the Pennine Way
Along the Roman Roads of Britain
Along the Green Roads of Britain
An Englishman's Home
Peel's England
All Over Britain
People and Places

1
Doone Land: Devon and Somerset

Brendon Two Gates stand a few miles east of The Chains, the bleakest tract on Exmoor, whence flowed the floods which in 1952 destroyed a large part of Lynmouth. It is true that the Ordnance Survey map marks Brendon Two Gates, but it is also true that you will never reach them, no matter how closely you follow the route thither. Arriving at the site – the border between Devon and Somerset – you will find only one gate, set there to serve livestock which cannot cross a cattle grid that has replaced the original gates which served as barriers against vagrant animals. The gates were so designed that a horseman could pass through without dismounting, whereafter the gates swung together again, barring the way. Sheep still graze beside the unfenced road, and sometimes they lie in the middle of it, but between October and June relatively few cars disturb them.

About a couple of miles north of Brendon Two Gates, on the right of the road, a track leads to the heart of the moor. It begins by climbing a ridge from which, glancing astern, you sight the confluence of the Severn Sea and the Atlantic Ocean, formerly a busy fairway, though now empty of anything except a few pleasure boats and coastal steamers. Beyond that ridge the track descends, and the high ground behind it creates a sound barrier, leaving you alone in a land of heather, grass, and silence. On the right, Withypool Ridge forms a treeless rampart which puzzles some people when they discover that the maps mark 'Exmoor Forest'. The word 'forest', however, used to mean any extensive tract of wild country, whether wooded or not. Mediaeval Exmoor Forest is said to have contained only two trees, Kite Oak and Hoar Oak.

After about a mile the track reaches the edge of Lank Combe, a deep and rocky ravine, with two domed summits in the background, each a thousand feet above the sea. When Richard Jefferies explored Exmoor, the area of uncultivated land was far greater than it is today. Jefferies, in fact, experienced an optical illusion, for, although he reckoned that he could reach a certain ridge within an hour, two hours' walking found him short of his destination because he had underestimated the distance and also the number of intervening combes that must be descended and then ascended. In his book *Red Deer* he admitted that the Exmoor terrain baffles a stranger: 'The country is very deceptive, much wider and more difficult than it looks . . . The expanse confuses the eye, and will not allow it to judge distances.'

Bearing north-west, the track passes a small signpost pointing to Bagworthy Water (moorfolk call it Badgery) and then turns south, along the tip of Lank Combe; then it crosses a stream with stepping stones: and after that it turns eastward again, climbing the side of Withycombe Ridge, past a solitary thorn tree that resembles Wordsworth's:

There is a Thorn – it looks so old,
In truth, you'd find it hard to say
How it could ever have been young,
It looks so old and grey.

Wherever you turn, you see only moorland and bare hills. Even the sheep are silent, though in summer the larks sing while a cuckoo answers its own echo from the combe. If you are lucky, you will sight a red stag, *Elephas cervans*, monarch of this its largest English habitat.

It is head-down now, climbing steeply yet never directly, because, like the stags, the track follows a devious course. Glancing behind and far below, you note that the thorn tree now seems no taller than a shrub, while sheep on the other side of Lank Combe might be mushrooms. In such a landscape it is not difficult to remember that mediaeval Exmoor was a royal chase or hunting ground whose boundaries were marked precisely. Verderers, or gamekeepers, protected pastures and deer ('The King's vert and venison'), and four Exmoor Courts sat every forty days, to try offenders against the forest laws. In return for attending those Courts, for maintaining the boundaries, and for supervising livestock, the moor's Free Suitors enjoyed certain rights, such as pasturage and peat-digging; the Suitors-at-Large, who performed no services, had to pay for such rights. Whether privileged or not, all moorfolk led a hard life, grubbing a meagre pittance from a grudging soil. When John Leland arrived in 1540 he did not like what he saw: 'Forest, barren and Morish ground', he reported, 'where is store and breading of young cattel, but little or no corne or habitation.'

The Crown eventually sold most of its land on the moor, chiefly to a few ancient families in Devon and Somerset. Since it no longer has an official boundary, we may say of Exmoor what W. H. Hudson said of Salisbury Plain, that it is not 'a precisely defined area, and may be made to include as much or as little as will suit the writer's purpose.' Continual reclamation by farmers has decimated the area of true moorland, and the destruction is irreparable because many centuries must elapse before an acre of reclaimed moorland reverts to its former state.

John Ridd, the hero of *Lorna Doone*, lived in this sector of Exmoor. His creator, Richard Doddridge Blackmore, first learned about the Doones when as a child he stayed with his grandfather, Rev. John Blackmore, at the Devon parsonage of the moorland parish in which I live. Whether the Doones ever did terrorise Exmoor is unknowable, though some people have tried to prove that the legends are based on fact. In 1901, for example, a Somerset newspaper published an article by 'Ida M. Browne (Audrie Doone)', claiming that the Doones really were outlawed Scottish aristocrats who had fled to Exmoor. The matter is interesting but not of prime importance. Like Kingsley's *Hereward the Wake*, Blackmore's *Lorna Doone* needs no verifiable prototype. In any event, books about the Doones had appeared long before Blackmore wrote his romance. In a preface to the 1869 edition of *Lorna Doone*, he acknowledged that every Exmoor man could recall 'the nurse-tales of his childhood – the savage deeds of the outlaw Doones in the depth of Bagworthy Forest . . . ' The legend certainly took root in his own youthful imagination, though not until he was middle-aged did he transmute the legend into a novel; and even then the book suffered a rough passage, being (as Blackmore revealed) 'rejected by all the best magazines, and publishers, and I felt *nearly* certain they were right.' Fortunately, he persevered and 'at last was fain to accept an offer of nothing for it'. In fact, Sampson Low published the book, on niggardly terms, after their literary advisers had wavered for more than a month. When it did appear, in 1869, it fell flat. 'Of the first 500 copies,' Blackmore explained, 'only about 300 were sold . . . ' That the novel revived and has ever since remained popular was due to a couple of coincidences, as follows: in 1870 one of Queen Victoria's daughters caused a stir by marrying a man who was not of royal blood, the Scottish Marquis of Lorne, whereupon a journalist announced that *Lorna Doone* told the truth about the Marquis's murderous ancestors. The effect of the announcement was immediate and dramatic; the public clamoured for Blackmore's neglected novel. Long after the wedding had ceased to be news, a sixpenny edition of the book sold 100,000 copies in six days, yet the author's royalties remained constant at less than £1 weekly. Three decades after the wedding, and six years after Blackmore's death, a class of Yale undergraduates chose *Lorna Doone* as their favourite novel, nine votes ahead of *Vanity Fair*.

En route to John Ridd's home, the track again alters course, plodding through silvery-grey grass; crossing a damp patch, aptly named Bogworth Lees; and descending to Hoccombe Combe and a small stream, a tributary of Bagworthy Water. On the left, among some stunted thorns, lies a ruined stone wall, an unexpected relic of humanity. The stream comes closer now, spanned by a bridge under gnarled oaks; after a few more yards Bagworthy Water appears, flowing through a narrow ravine whose far side is so steep that you must crick your neck in order to see the sheep on the summit. Bagworthy Water at this point is a series of miniature cascades, confirming Southey's remark that every Exmoor stream enters 'a combe, rolling over huge stones like a long waterfall'. It was somewhere on these upper reaches that John, while still a child, went fishing for trout. 'The covert,' he remembered, 'grew darker above me, until I thought that the fishes might have a good chance of eating me, instead of my eating the fishes.' Advancing deeper into the ravine, he reached 'a great dark pool' and there he nearly drowned. On recovering consciousness, he saw 'a little girl at my side, rubbing my forehead tenderly with a dock leaf and a handkerchief.' John Ridd had met Lorna Doone.

The site of that meeting is as vague as the site of John's home, Plover's Barrow Farm. At Malmsmead, a few miles downstream, a gift shop has claimed to occupy the site, but the shop itself is only a few yards from Bagworthy Water, whereas John said that the Water was hardly visible from the house. The rest of his description could fit several other Exmoor farms: 'How pleasant and soft the fall of the land is round Plover's Barrow Farm. All above it is strong dark mountain, spread with heath, and desolate, but near our house . . . open warmth and shelter. Here are trees and bright green grass, and orchards full of contentment . . . ' The editor of Baedeker's *Handbook to*

Great Britain was so puzzled by what he called 'the discrepancy between the actual scenery of the Doone Valley and the description of it in *Lorna Doone*' that he questioned Blackmore, who replied: 'If I had dreamed that it would ever be more than a book of the moment, the descriptions of the scenery – which I know as well as my own garden – would have kept nearer the fact.' Blackmore was justified in saying that he knew the moor intimately. Like John Ridd, he had received a classical West Country education at Blundell's School in Tiverton; unlike John Ridd, he graduated at Exeter College, Oxford, another West Country foundation. As a child he explored the moor, sometimes on foot, sometimes on a pony. In the preface to *Tales from a Telling House* he painted an endearing portrait of himself and his grandfather going the rounds of their North Devon parish: 'I behold an old man, with a keen profile, under a parson's shovel hat, riding a tall chestnut horse up the western slope of Exmoor, followed by his little grandson upon a shaggy and stuggy pony . . . Some four or five miles behind them may be seen the ancient Parsonage, where the lawn is a russet sponge of moss and a stream tinkles under the dining room floor . . . ' The parsonage – now a guesthouse – has not greatly altered since Blackmore stayed there.

Were I a betting man I would wager a considerable sum that, between mid-October and early June, you could follow this sector of Bagworthy Water on six consecutive days, without meeting anyone. Since it lies at no great distance from my home, I walk this way several times each year, and only thrice during the past decade have I seen anyone near Blackmore's 'great dark pool'. The scene composes a symphony of those sounds – a bird, a brook, a sheep, a stag – which we call stillness. Thomas Hood caught the timbre with a single line: 'Here the true silence is, self-conscious and alone."

Blackmore's novel long ago caused this sector of Bagworthy Water to be dubbed 'The Doone Valley'. Even the Ordnance Survey marks it 'Doone Country'. Of the visitors who do drive to Malmsmead, one wonders how many have ever read *Lorna*

Doone, and what their response would be if they did read it. Blackmore, after all, was a Victorian, a Christian, a Conservative, a scholar. He eulogised Freud's Super-Ego, but seldom analysed the Id. In a preface to the sixth edition he expressed his pleasure that *Lorna Doone* had 'entered many a happy, pure, and hospitable home.' In his own life he strove toward the light as he saw it, and Eden Phillpotts, who evoked Dartmoor as vividly as Blackmore evoked Exmoor, said of him: 'He showed – as every supreme artist has shown – that goodness is man's only hope; that evil, sooner or later, reaps the whirlwind . . . Those who knew him can attest how those qualities of fearlessness and modesty and respect for the wonderful gift entrusted to his keeping were part of himself . . . His manliness, insight, glorious humour, were a tonic to the mind . . . '

The high peaks of Exmoor overlook the Severn Sea and the Glamorganshire coast, where Blackmore spent part of his childhood. Those early years serve as a reminder that he wrote several novels and tales about Wales, one of which, *The Maid of Skerne*, he rated above *Lorna Doone*, an opinion which was shared by Sir Hall Caine, himself a talented novelist. Like several other prose writers, Blackmore in his youth wrote verse, but his *Poems by Melander* were never more than graceful. Many years later, however, a poem came to him in a dream, about the recent death of a relative: this was published under his initials, in *The University Magazine*, where it was entitled *Dominus Illuminatio Mea* (In Memoriam M.E.G.). This title, meaning 'The Lord is my Light', is the motto of Blackmore's University. Sir Arthur Quiller-Couch, who either discovered or received a copy of the poem, with the initials omitted, liked it so much that he chose it as the final poem in *The Oxford Book of English Verse*. Nine years later, when Blackmore was dead, a letter in *The Athenaeum* revealed the poet's name. Blackmore's biographer, Professor Waldo H. Dunn, wrote: 'Many poets have said they would be satisfied if they could be remembered by a dozen lines. Blackmore has gained immortality with sixteen.' The first stanza enshrines

Blackmore's *credo*:

> In the hour of death, after this life's whim,
> When the heart beats low, and the eyes grow dim,
> And pain has exhausted every limb –
> The lover of the Lord shall trust in Him.

For most people, however, Blackmore's fame rests on one book, *Lorna Doone*, which, although it has been mocked by several twentieth-century critics, was admired by scholars no less percipient than I. A. Richards and F.R. Leavis. Bred on the Bible and on the Greek and Latin classics, Blackmore wrote prose which may sound over-rich to readers who were reared on a diet of gruel. Even his modern admirers admit that he sometimes indulged a degree of sentiment which now seems excessive; yet it is idle to chide a Victorian for being a Victorian; not Shakespeare himself has spanned every yard of the centuries. *Lorna Doone* is among those books that Sir Philip Sidney classified as 'A tale which holdeth children from play, and old men from the chimney corner.' Not to have read it, is not to have understood the extent to which the people and places of Exmoor remain recognisable as those whom John Ridd knew three centuries ago.

A footpath follows Bagworthy Water downstream, keeping to high ground on the left. When the path descends, the combe widens and eventually enters a green glade whose seclusion is heightened because the combe's steep sides foreshorten the view ahead. There are several monuments to the man who made that view famous. As an Anglican, he would approve the mural in Oare church, where Carver Doone shot Lorna while she was being married to John. As a Conservative who admired whatever to him seemed admirable in the Establishment, he would approve the statue and a memorial window in Exeter Cathedral. As a countryman of North Devon lineage, he would approve – might, indeed, prize above all – the monument beside the path at a point where the glade widens. There, on the left, stands a handsome stone plinth 'To the memory of RDB whose novel *Lorna Doone* extols to all the joys of Exmoor'.

2
Off the Beaten Track: Buckinghamshire

The postman had been right when he warned me that the place was hard to find. I began the journey at Prestwood, two miles from Great Missenden, following a footpath through Monument Lodge Wood and then entering the narrow valley at Little Hampden. By climbing the right-hand side of the valley, I joined a path through the beechwoods to Dunsmore, walking leisurely, for it was early afternoon in October, and my destination lay only a mile or two beyond Dunsmore; but Dunsmore itself detained me, so unexpected it was, a hamlet in a wood on a hill. Since I had only recently begun to explore the Chilterns, even a short walk revealed pleasant surprises; a cottage in a wood on a hill, or a pond in a wood on a hill, or a prehistoric highway in a wood on a hill. As the postman remarked: 'It's all 'ills 'ere.'

At Dunsmore I found a small shop, a small inn, and about a dozen cottages, one of which – Daffodil Cottage – seemed almost too small to enter. Nobody appeared. The entire population (it may have been sixty) was either indoors or away from home. Some of the cottages were scattered at random among trees, linked by a footpath with a stile. For ten minutes I sat on the stile, in a stillness so profound that a robin, breaking suddenly into song, quite startled me. I did hear a door being opened, and after that I did hear a cat mewing. The rest was silence.

From Dunsmore I followed a lane downhill, overlooking a wide valley crowned by beechwoods. At the foot of the lane I reached Little London, which proved to be less a place than a place-name; and still nobody appeared. Presently the sound of a distant train told me that I was more or less on course. Sure enough, the narrow lane sent out an even narrower one which eventually joined a lane that may have been a yard wider. Two handsome brick-and-flint houses confirmed my navigation, for at that point the postman had told me to turn left. I lingered awhile, admiring the houses; but when the sun sank behind a hill I knew that I must either turn back or risk losing myself among unfamiliar woods. On second thoughts, having come so far, I decided not to give up. At a brisk pace, therefore, I continued along the lane, which soon became a track; and on the track I paused just long enough to glimpse what I had come to see. Then I hurried back, hoping to find the way before nightfall could hide it.

A few days later I returned to the track, at about the same hour as before, but this time by car in frosty weather. Leaving the car in the lane, I followed the track, a wide and grassy one, flanked by many trees. After a few hundred yards I reached my destination, an inn. Being in no hurry, I walked past the place, climbing to a rampart of beechwoods that stretched at least four miles, from the edge of Batcombe Wood near Wendover to the edge of Hampdenleaf Wood near Great Missenden. The track meanwhile delved deeper and steeper into silence. Somewhere a robin sang the final note of a belated Evensong; somewhere else a squirrel scurried through the fallen leaves. Then silence returned, heightened by the sound of my own footsteps rustling a copper-coloured carpet of innumerable autumns. It was certainly the same season, and might have been the same place, which W. Kean Seymour described:

> Only the small faint stir of leaves that fall,
> And the pure music of a robin's flute,
> Invade the sense with sound: all else is mute,
> A fane of dreams most still and magical.

As I returned downhill, the inn's lamplit window shone like a glowworm through trees. The inn itself was a cottage, more like a private than a public house. Entering, I found myself in a small living-room, where an old man sat beside the fire. He did not move, but stared at me, impassive as a Buddha. His dew-lapped cheeks were pasty, and on his head he wore a black skullcap.

'Where,' I asked, 'is the bar?'

'Here,' he replied.

Feeling as though I had entered a stranger's home uninvited, I said: 'I'll take a glass of cider.'

'Cider.' The publican repeated the word, not quite as a question, nor wholly as a statement, nor utterly as a rebuke, but partaking of all three. Rising from his chair, he shuffled to a corner of the room, where a hole in the floor revealed a steep stairway to the cellar, from whose depth he called: 'Any particular cider?'

'Sweet, preferably.'

'Sweet.' Again the old man's voice hovered between indifference and disapproval.

Above the clink of bottles, I heard him wheezing. Then, very slowly, his skullcap reappeared, as though rising from a trap door.

'Sweet cider,' he stated.

'Thank you.' I replied.

It really was a living-room, with table, chairs, radio, knitting basket, and various family nicknacks. Having paid, I sat down and was silent. After a while it occurred to me that the old man's uncouthness was (as Dr. Johnson expressed it) 'in his manners, not in his mind'. I therefore said: 'This seems a very remote spot for an inn.'

'Not nowadays. They've all got cars or motor bikes. Besides, we're only a few miles from Halton.'

'Halton?'

'Air Force.'

'I didn't hear any aircraft.'

'You won't. Halton's a non-flying place, thank God, so we're able to lead a civilised existence. Anyway, when this cottage first became a pub the farmers still employed a lot of men. Now it's all machines.' He spat into the beech logs. 'Have you come far?'

'From Prestwood.'

'I didn't hear a car.'

'I left it in the lane.'

At that moment a woman appeared, younger than the man and more cordial. Having said good evening, she began to lay the table. Still feeling less than at ease, I drank the cider and went away.

Three months later I returned and was again the only customer. Noticing that I stared at his skullcap, the old man said: 'I've just washed my hair.' From another room the woman laughed: 'He's very vain.' When she came in to lay the table, I left, not wishing to intrude on their evening meal.

My next visit occurred a year later, on a night so dark and drenching that I risked driving the car along the track. This time the old man was surprised to see me. 'Made a special journey?' he asked.

'No. I happened to be in Wendover, so I turned off at Little London.'

The silence was audible. Only the clock spoke, tick-tocking from a ledge above the fire, and sometimes a fragment of log tinkling in the hearth. The solitude was likewise perceptible, encompassed by hills and woods. It would not have been difficult to suppose that London was a hundred miles and a hundred years away.

'Wendover?' The old man turned my statement into a belated question. 'It's all motor cars there.' Again he spat into the fire. 'When I were a nipper it was all horses, except for a bus that used to break down. You could hear yourself speak in them days. Wendover!' He spat a third time. 'I stay at home, that's what I do. It's quiet here, except Saturday nights in the summer. I prefer the winter, like what it is now. Quiet.'

Presently the woman appeared, carrying a teapot, which reminded the publican that he had not yet taken my order. 'Sweet cider?' he asked.

'I'd rather have tea,' I replied, whereupon the woman fetched a third cup and saucer.

'Just hark at that rain,' the publican muttered. 'There won't be anyone in tonight. Not except Arnold. He never fails on Friday. I've known him come when the drifts were six feet high. A good customer is Arnold.'

'Does he live near?'

The publican nodded vaguely over his shoulder and then at the clock. 'Another three minutes and you'll see him.'

On the fifth stroke of eight, the door opened, the curtains quivered, and a man entered, his oilskin gleaming. I set him as early middle-aged, of medium height, midway between plain-faced and pleasant-featured. When he removed the oilskin, I saw that he wore a Norfolk jacket, cord breeches, fawn stockings, black brogues. Without being asked, the woman went down to the cellar, returning with a pint of beer.

'What a night,' the newcomer remarked.

'But it'd take more than the rain to keep *you* away,' the woman replied.

'Good health to all,' he wished, raising the tankard.

'And to you, Arnold,' the publican nodded.

No introduction was made, so I sat listening. Arnold's voice and manner suggested that he was a farmer rather than a gamekeeper; probably the tenant of a small property. I cannot now remember what he discussed, but I feel certain that the topics were rural and local. After a while I left.

Again a year passed; again I called; again Arnold was the

only other customer. This time he spoke of rabbits in Batcombe Warren; of Hildreth, the Prestwood tailor, a keen cricketer, whom he knew by name; of the price of eggs at Thame Market; and of a fox that had massacred ten chickens at Little Hampden. Before leaving, I said to the publican: 'I've made several visits here, and on each occasion you've just washed your hair.' By way of reply, the old man grinned at Arnold, removed his skullcap, and exposed a completely bald scalp.

'I told you he was vain,' the woman laughed.

Another twelve months passed, and then I called once more, and was again the only customer until, at eight o'clock, Arnold arrived, this time accompanied by his small son, whose costume was a replica of the father's, except that the boy's shoes were not brogues. Arnold himself was carrying a gun, which he set carefully against the grandfather clock. I never discovered Arnold's surname, nor his occupation, nor where he lived; and after a few minutes I departed, walking home through starless woods whose paths I now knew so well that I could have followed them by the sound of their fallen leaves and by the tug of their various contours. All that occurred nearly half a century ago.

Last year I returned to the inn, arriving at ten o'clock on a bright May morning; but instead of savouring the quietude, I endured the drone of aircraft and the rumble of traffic from a distant road that had become a commercial race-track. Although Little London and the narrow lane looked much the same as when I first saw them, I never did reach the inn, and I never shall. It had vanished under a grassy grave. Only by looking at the trees could I tell that the Leathern Bottle once stood there.

3
Ultima Thule: Caithness and Sutherland

I began to wonder whether anyone ever did use the road, or ever had, or ever would. Actually, I was walking from John o' Groat's to Land's End, walking steadily yet without haste, for I proposed to cover not less than twenty miles each day; to rest on Sundays; to follow (when it was possible) footpaths and minor roads via the Welsh mountains; to stop and stare (when it seemed appropriate) at vistas and castles and sunsets; and to go somewhat out of my way in order to visit a church, or a harbour, or a battlefield. In no sense was I competing against the people who travel as quickly as maybe, seeing as little as possible. I wished to see as much as possible, and for that reason the journey lasted from late March until mid-May. Meanwhile, my immediate destination was Forsinard, which, so I understood, comprised a railway line, a few planks posing as a station, and a small hotel.

After what seemed an eternity of solitude, I sighted a croft, set back from the road. Having already shared more than enough of my own company, I hailed the elderly man who was working among his vegetables: no proper sanitation, he told me, no telephone, no electricity. When I asked for how many hours a day he worked, he replied: 'Twenty-five.' That meeting occurred thirty years ago. The crofter, therefore, is dead; and his successors enjoy a less Spartan routine.

At the end of a silent and solitary afternoon, with the March sunlight looking as though it would soon fade, I reached those planks; but of the rest of Forsinard I could find no trace at all, except one house. With visions of a hot bath and a high tea, I approached the house, guessing that it was the hotel. Even from a distance the place wore a vacant expression. Peering through a window, I saw tables and chairs stacked upside-down beside an empty hearth. Five minutes later, after repeated peerings and knockings, I returned to the railway line, though I knew that no train would stop there until the morning. Why, it may be asked, had I not reserved a room at the hotel? The answer is simple: at John o' Groat's they had assured me that there was no need to do so. 'Forsinard,' they said, 'will have plenty of room. At this time of year you may be the only guest.' Having, then, drawn a blank, I considered the situation and did not like it because the light was fading fast, the temperature had dropped, and my legs declared that in no circumstance would they walk to the nearest other hotel, almost twenty miles away. Scanning the sky, I remembered that during the journey from Euston I had seen snow on the Perthshire mountains. Moreover, I was near the Fairy Hillocks (an ironic name), a region famed for its blizzards. In 1895 a goods train was snowbound, only a few miles from where I now stood. Admittedly, the crew managed to reach a cottage, but the train was buried under the drifts, and ten days passed before it was found and dug out by a gang of one hundred men. I began to wish that I had followed Daniel Defoe's advice to travellers in Caithness, bidding them 'Go with some company, and carrying tents . . . so encamping every night as if it were an army.' My own encampment seemed likely to be made without a tent.

While unpacking the iron rations, I decided that very few isolated hotels are left completely empty while their rivals have already opened their doors to Easter visitors. I therefore went back, hoping to find signs of habitation, if only a loaf on the kitchen table or a milk bottle at the back door. This time, even before I had knocked, I heard someone sawing logs. To cut a short story shorter, John o' Groat's had misled me. The Forsinard hotel was not due to open until the following week. Nevertheless, despite my premature arrival, a fire was lit in the dining-room, the boiler was stoked, a bed was prepared, a meal was cooked; and at nine o'clock, having walked twenty miles since breakfast, I fell asleep.

Next morning I awoke to the same blue skies that had greeted the nineteenth-century American blacksmith, Elihu Burritt, when he, too, reached Caithness on foot: 'A lark was soaring and warbling,' he wrote, 'with as happy and hopeful a voice as if he were singing over the greenest acres of any English meadow.' On the next lap of my journey to Helmsdale, the landscape was most unlike an English meadow, for it contained very few trees, very few birds, and such a paucity of people that I walked a dozen miles without seeing anyone, all the while surrounded by bald hills, rocky outcrops, marshy valleys. My knowledge of botany and geology being soon expended, I tried to recall what I knew of Caithness itself, the northernmost county on the British mainland, anciently called *Ultima Thule* or 'The End of the World'. Many Englishfolk regard the extreme north of Scotland as more Scottish than the south of Scotland, but it is not so. In Caithness, for example, less than one percent of the population speak Gaelic, whereas in Ross and Cromarty, away to the south, the percentage of Gaelic-speakers is thirty-five. This disparity is not surprising when you reflect that Caithness was for centuries dominated by Denmark, and that the Orkneys were Danish territory (in the Shetlands the word *okregord* or 'arable field' comes from the Old Danish *akkagaror*). When Norsemen conquered Caithness, eleven centuries ago, they found there a Pictish people whose name, *Catti*, implied that they were as ferocious as wild cats, whence the name *Katanes* or Caithness, meaning 'Cat-promontory'. The Scandinavian influence spread as far south as Fife, where Boswell and Dr. Johnson met a man who told then about 'a colony of Danes in his parish; that they had landed at a remote period of time, and still remained a distinct people.' Whether true or not, the story proves the longevity of Danish influence on Scotland.

When at last I did sight a house, I admired the stamina of the crofters who lived among miles of peat, aeons of rock, and very few neighbours. Even more admirable was the self-reliance of crofters who settled there before the isolation had been mitigated by railways, telephones, cars, radio, aircraft. Unless they wrote a letter, or either made or received a visit, such people had no means of knowing how their friends fared, over the hills and ten miles away.

The population of Caithness is so small – about the same as Melton Mowbray's – that the houseless horizons suggest an illimitable distance. Despite its bleakness, however, Caithness contains the largest area of potential farmland north of Dornoch Firth; a fact which was recorded by Thomas Pennant, one of the few eighteenth-century travellers who ventured into *Ultima Thule*: 'Caithness,' he observed, 'may be called an immense morass, mixed with some fruitful spots of oats and barley . . . ' The county's Cheviot sheep are a legacy from Sir John Sinclair, founder of the Board of Agriculture, who imported the breed from England during the eighteenth century. The Sinclairs prove that, despite Scandinavian influence, Caithness adopted the Scottish clan system (the name of another Caithness clan, the Gunn, is a variant of the Old Norse *gunnr* or 'war').

At John o' Groat's I had assumed that the end-of-the-worldness would recede as I went south. The assumption was mistaken. No matter where I turned, I saw only coarse grass, grey rock, bald hills, vast swamps, houseless skylines; a prospect which confirmed what the maps had already emphasised, that in northern Scotland, if you do not like the road you have chosen, you are at liberty to walk twenty trackless miles in search of a better one. Daunted by the size of India, Britons see their own country as a mere speck, and its mainland does indeed look small when compared with the rest of Europe. However, when compared with the rest of the kingdom, the British mainland looks very large indeed, and to me, southward bound for Cornwall, it appeared immense. The train from Euston had taken a whole day to reach Glasgow, where I boarded a train for Perth, arriving late at night. Early next morning I took a train to Wick, once more travelling most of the day, and once more changing, this time to a bus that reached John o' Groat's about nine o'clock at night. Never again did I regard the British mainland as a mere speck.

Some time during the afternoon my boots began to pinch, not because they had suddenly shrunk but because the ankles had gradually swollen. The road at that point was flanked on the left by high ground, from which a cascade of water splashed on to a brook. I therefore halted, removed the boots and socks, and plunged both feet into the icy bath: and there I rested, like the man in the old song:

> I sits with my feet in a brook;
> If anyone asks me for why,
> I hits him a whack with my crook
> . . . 'It's sentiment kills me,' says I.

On reflection, the analogy is only half valid, for no one questioned my conduct, nor, even had he done so, would I have struck him with my walking stick; and in any event it was wisdom, not sentiment, that caused me to seek the therapeutic properties of water. Five minutes later the boots felt comfortable again, which was as well because the blue sky showed several dark clouds approaching from the north. This change of weather surprised me, though not so much as did the man who suddenly appeared round a bend in the road, followed by a dog. The man's face showed that he was at least as surprised as myself.

'Does anyone ever use this road?' I asked.

'I do,' the man replied. 'And sometimes the folk at Forsinard.'

'Was it always so deserted?'

'No, indeed.' He glanced over his shoulder. 'On yon brae there used to be a shooting lodge. It employed quite a few men, aye, and some lasses, too. But nowadays the lairds are taxed till their houses fall down.'

'You come from the Highlands,' I suggested.

'Pairth,' he agreed. 'Forty years ago.' Again he glanced at the brae. 'My sister worked at yon lodge. She . . . you canna' see the place, it's only a pile o' stones . . . she found me a job there.'

Noticing that he held himself erect despite the years, I said: 'Were you a soldier?'

Instantly his chin jutted a full three inches in the air. 'Gordon Highlanders,' he replied. 'Seventeen years. The best of my life with the best of my friends.' Slowly his chin descended. 'But that was a long time ago.' He stared at my pack. 'You're on a tour, no doubt?'

'You could say so, yes.'

'And the wee dog?'

'Where I go, he goes.'

'I've met a mort o' bad men, but verra few bad dogs.' He studied the spaniel. 'Well-bred,' he decided. 'Costly, in fact. Working?'

'Only when I go rabbiting.'

'Even rabbits are better than a stroll round the park. Yon dog was bred to work.' Now he glanced at the sky, where a black cloud had seeped into the grey.

'Snow?' I wondered.

'It could be. 'Tis only March month, mind.'

'So you think I ought to be moving.'

'And mesel', too. I've some sheep to tend afore I make for hame. Hae a guid walk.'

'I'll try to.'

With that brief hail and farewell we went our ways; he northward to the sheep, I southward to the sea; by which time the clouds had proliferated, an ominous sign during a season when snow was likely. At four miles an hour I continued into the solitude that unfolded all around, from the soggy plain astern to the soggy valley ahead. Some time later I heard a train in the valley, ambling to Thurso, devious as a serpent avoiding the swamps. The first line in these parts was the Sutherland Railway, which tried to reach Brora, a coal-mining village on the coast, but could not afford to do so, whereupon the Duke of Sutherland formed his own company in 1871, carrying the line from Golspie to Helmsdale, a distance of seventeen miles. At about the same time, Elihu Burritt reported an event that would soon turn the Highlands into a playground: 'The railway from Perth to Inverness via Dunkeld and Blair Atholl has just opened up this secluded Scotch Switzerland to multitudes.' In 1874 the Sutherland and Caithness Railway reached Wick. On my own northward journey I had reckoned that the line from Inverness to Wick covered one hundred and sixty miles whereas the road covered only one hundred and forty. The difference was caused by the railway's need to serve as many potential passengers as possible, and since most of them lived in small seaside settlements, the line followed the indented coast.

At teatime, when the last patch of blue sky vanished, I rested long enough to sip some coffee, thereafter maintaining a steady pace, as though forewarned by Burritt: 'For a long distance,' he wrote, 'the country was exceedingly wild and desolate. Terrible must be the condition of a man benighted therein, especially in winter.' Although the scenery was as wild as ever, the road began to descend, and I knew that I had entered Sutherland, only a few miles from my destination. Sutherland or 'Southland' seems a strange name for the second most northerly county on the mainland; in fact, the name implies that the county lies along the southern edge of Caithness. By whatever name, Sutherland is wilder than Caithness and its population even smaller, being about 13,000 people in an area of more than a million acres (the average British population per square mile is 586; in Sutherland it is seven). Most of the county is a wilderness of mountains and streams, teeming with roe deer and red deer. The Earls of Sutherland led a quasi-regal life. Burritt described the contemporary Duke as 'the largest land-owner in Great Britain and probably Europe'. Sir William Fraser's *Sutherland Book* was more specific, stating that in 1892 the Duke 'purchased from Eric, Lord Reay, the whole of the Reay County . . . He also at different times acquired the following lands: the estate of Bighouse, from Major Colin Mackay; the barony of Skelbo, in the parish of Creich; the lands of Armadale and Strathy, in the barony of Farr; the barony of Torboll; the lands of Uppat near Dunrobin; the estate of Carrol in the parish of Clyne . . . ' Fraser continued the litany: 'the estate of Ardross with fishings on the Shin; part of the Kyles of Oykel and the Dornoch Firth; the lands of Iveran, from Macleod of Cadboll; with the superiority of the burgh of Wick and certain properties in Dornoch. Besides these purchased by the first Duke, his son, the second Duke, prior to 1835 purchased the lands of Creich, also the lands of Langwell, being part of the Skibo estate, another part of the same estate, Sandycroft or Captain's Park, being acquired by an excambion with Mr. Dempster of Skibo; likewise the lands of Teabreck, near Tain, and the lands of Embo, with various properties in the burghs of Tain, Wick, and Dornoch.'

To me at that time both Sutherland and Caithness were *terra incognita*, but when I returned thither and was able to explore them leisurely, I admired the barren mountains of the former and the flat fertility of the latter. Above all, I relished the companionable isolation of John o' Groat's, finding there a camaraderie of crofting-fisherfolk whose whitewashed cottages and farmhouses clustered near the edge of the cliff, leading a communal life of their own (the local dramatic society has won first prize in a festival at which the whole of Scotland competed).

I had now been on the road for nearly eight hours, and in all that time I saw two cars and one pedestrian. It was therefore with some curiosity that I entered Helmsdale, a pleasant little town beside the river of that name, which forms the boundary with Caithness. Writing in the first century AD, Ptolemy called the river the *Ila* (the Gaels still do call it the *Ilidh*). In a tributary of the Helmsdale, the Suigill Burn, gold was found, which created a brief Victorian gold-rush; but there was no kind of rush when I arrived. Three cars were parked there, outside a shop; and in the street I counted three people. Having secured a room at the hotel, I strolled down to the harbour. Only one vessel was there – a small coaster, beached high and dry – and only one sailor, tarring a dinghy in the sunset.

'Not much shipping,' I remarked.

'Not much,' the sailor agreed. 'But many vessels called here when I was a bairn. Aye, and we'd many fishing boats, too.'

If he is still alive, that sailor will have witnessed a revival, sufficient to bring more than one vessel and one dinghy; but I doubt that anybody will ever again see what Burritt saw at Helmsdale: 'a vigorous, bustling busy fishing village nestling under the shadow of the mountains at the mouth of the little river . . . After tea, went down to the wharf or quay and had some conversation with one of the masters of the business. He cured and put up about 30,000 barrels of herrings himself in a season, employing, while it lasted, 500 persons . . . this little sea-side village imported . . . their salt from Liverpool, their staves from Norway, and their hoops from London.'

Back at the hotel, I received a welcome as warm as Forsinard's. The high tea offered a choice of fish or of ham and eggs, with three kinds of bread, home-baked scones, honey, jam, and a fruit cake. Afterwards, in the small lounge, the dog basked beside the fire, well-groomed, well-fed, well-pleased. He must have walked and hunted at least thirty miles during the day, and since I had walked about twenty, I was ready for bed at nine o'clock, and would have retired thither had not two men entered and said 'Good evening' so cordially that, after an almost speechless day, I decided to linger awhile. The men, I learned, were father and son, aged about seventy and thirty. On hearing the nature of my journey, the son said: 'Lucky those clouds went away this afternoon. I thought we were in for some snow. And believe me, when it does snow . . . well, men have died on that road to Forsinard.'

'Do you,' I asked, 'go there yourself?'

'For my sins, yes. I'm a sales rep.'

'Have you ever been snowbound?'

'Damned nearly. If I hadn't carried chains I'd have been forced to walk back, and in that weather I'd have been lucky to cover half a mile.'

Just then I noticed that the father was winking at me, which seemed inexplicable until he gave his own account of the road, as follows: the son had lately taken over part of the territory which his father had served as a commercial traveller in 1906: 'And in those years,' the veteran said, 'the road really was hazardous. You,' he turned affectionately to his son, 'you travel in a warm car, and almost every house you pass has a telephone. But I travelled in a pony and trap, and none of the houses had a telephone. If it was snowing the day before I reached Helmsdale, I'd try to get a message to Forsinard, "If I haven't arrived by such-and-such a time", I told them, "come out and look for me." '

'Did they ever need to?' I asked.

'No, but I was once caught in the drifts. I unharnessed the pony, and he carried me to the nearest croft. It was several days before I could get away.'

At nine-thirty I excused myself, saying: 'If I don't go now, I shall fall asleep on the stairs.'

At nine-forty I did fall asleep, in the warm bed and to the sound of the sea.

4
The Spirit of Delight: Sussex

I was trying to find a house which lay so far off the beaten track that one of its former occupants drew a map to guide his friends thither. This elusive place stood near Fittleworth, four miles south of Petworth, on the boundary between the South Downs and the Weald or Wild, a forest which covered much of mediaeval Sussex and parts of Kent and Surrey and Hampshire. In 1586 William Camden mentioned 'an opinion that some men maintain concerning this Weald, which is, that it was a great while together in manner nothing else than a desert and waste wilderness, not planted with towns or peopled with men, as the outsides of the shire were, but stored and stuffed with herds of deer and droves of hogs only'. In Camden's day the forest was already being destroyed by industrialists: 'It is,'

he reported, 'full of mines, for the casting of iron of which there are furnaces up and down the country, and abundance of wood is yearly spent . . . .' Sussex still contains so many woods that one tends to forget the extent of their destruction by industrialists. At Beckley, for example, near the village of Brede, I discovered a cluster of cottages with a Furnace House, a Furnace Lane, and in the woods the wheel of a ruined watermill. During the Civil War this small factory made cannon for the rebel armies, thereby creating the kind of din which offended Camden: 'The hammers beating on the iron,' he complained, 'fill the neighbourhood round about, night and day, with continued noise.' During the eighteenth century the factory made guns, firelocks, fire-irons, brand-irons, and brass skillets; but in 1770 it was closed because pit coal had become cheaper than charcoal. A bitter denunciation of the Sussex iron-masters appeared in Michael Drayton's verse travelogue, *Poly-Olbion*, where the trees speak for themselves:

> These iron times breed none that mind posterity,
> 'Tis but vain to tell what we have been before.

Drayton showed the industrialists as selfishly squandering the nation's resources while posing as public benefactors:

> When under public good, base private greed takes hold,
> And we, poor woeful trees, to ruin lastly sold.

Industry was as greedy then as it is now. In 1610 Sussex had 140 forges which burned 80,000 trees every year. King James I was warned that the royal forests contained only 350,000 trees, less than half of them fit for ship-building. Such destruction could not be made good by natural regeneration, nor was there then a policy of national afforestation. Pepys and Evelyn, both of whom were Admiralty officials, tried to curb the industrialists. Evelyn, in fact, wrote a book, *Sylva, or a discourse of Forest-trees and the propagation of Timber in H.M.'s Dominions*, which proved so effective that the Battle of Trafalgar was said to have been won in his study near the naval dockyards at Deptford.

During the next century William Gilpin counted the cost of the destruction: 'Some of the noblest oaks in England were formerly found in Sussex. They required sometimes a score of oxen to draw them, and were carried in a sort of wain, which in that deep country is expressively called a tugg.' The journey from Sussex to the dockyards went leisurely: 'Two or three years was not an uncommon space of time for a tree to spend in performing its journey to Chatham. One tugg carried the load but a little way, and left it for another tugg to take up. If the rains set in it stirred no more that year . . . ' Coal could have been used instead of wood, but it was more expensive, so the destruction continued. When a relatively cheap coal-burning furnace was invented, the industrialists stopped felling, thus depriving many Sussex labourers of employment. By that time, however, the damage was irreparable, and the last Wealden furnace closed down at Ashburton in 1828.

The Weald, then, had been more than decimated when Sir Edward Elgar – who once occupied Brinkwells, the elusive cottage that I was seeking – went to live near Fittleworth; yet Sussex was still a quiet and relatively secluded county (in 1903 E. V. Lucas described it as 'delectable and inaccessible'). Commuters scarcely existed, cars were few, aircraft were almost unknown. Horses and bicycles and steam trains remained the principal modes of travel. Brinkwells had been discovered by Elgar's wife and their daughter in 1917, when he himself was more than usually ill and depressed, for the war appalled him, he loathed London ('I am sick of towns,' he wrote), and his music had failed to win the wide recognition which he craved. To those current stresses were added several from the past. Like Thomas Hardy, Elgar was born the son of a tradesman at a time when social differences were sharper than they are today. A woman who knew him while he was young remarked that his parentage and upbringing caused him to feel 'a humiliation so cruel and so crushing that he could not bear even to speak of it'. One thinks of the bitterness which Charles Dickens felt whenever he recalled his own sense of shame as a child who had been sent to work in a London factory; yet one thinks also of those other men who, rising from humble circumstances to eminence, mixed confidently and amicably with all classes of society, and were proud, not ashamed, of their own background. Again like Hardy, Elgar had exacerbated the matter by marrying above himself, his bride being the daughter of a major-general whose family would have nothing to do with an unknown musician, the son of a shopkeeper. The bride's father died long before his daughter's marriage, but her aunts subsequently cut the couple out of the Will which could have given them financial security. Always poor and sometimes desperately so, Elgar was forced to waste time and energy on giving violin lessons. When he was past forty years old and had written some of the finest English music since Purcell, he told his friend, August Jaeger: 'I want so little . . . £300 a year . . . Last year I subsisted on £200.' The next sentence spoke for innumerable artists down the centuries: 'It seems strange that a man who might do good work should be absolutely stopped . . . ' In fact, he never was stopped; on the contrary, he achieved an honorary Cambridge degree, the Mastership of the King's Musick, a baronetcy, and the Order of Merit. Moreover, several leading musicologists worked assiduously to proclaim and perform his music. Nevertheless, at the age of sixty-four, Elgar could still distort the truth by saying: 'As a child and as a young man and as a mature man, no single person has ever helped me.' His complaint was ungrammatical as well as ungrateful, and it implied a psychological malaise.

Such, then, was the man, and such his mood, who in 1917 acquired the lease of a country cottage. Fourteen years earlier, E. V. Lucas had observed: 'Fittleworth has of late become an artists' Mecca, partly because of its pretty woods and quaint architecture, and partly because of the welcome that is offered by the "Swan" . . . ' The Elgars' cottage certainly lay off the beaten track, some distance from Fittleworth village, which itself was so secluded that E. V. Lucas wondered whether he would ever reach the inn there: 'Approaching it from the north it seems to be the end of all things . . . ' Elgar loved Brinkwells at first sight. 'It is divine,' he told Leo Frank Schuster, 'a simple thatched cottage . . . with wonderful views.' For another friend, W. H. Reed, he sketched a map to guide him on his way from Pulborough. The route (marked as 'Reed's route thus') leads south-west toward a signpost which Elgar drew as a finger, pointing to the River Arun and 'Bridge 15th Century'. After about a mile the map shows an arrow, pointing north ('Turn here'). The word 'TREES' appears on each side of the track; on the left, Elgar added an unflattering caricature of himself and his dog. Finally, surrounded by more trees, he drew Brinkwells, with its chimney emitting 'Smoke of WELCOME'.

I have visited Brinkwells twice, each time by invitation (it is a private residence, not a public museum). The privacy is enhanced by the difficulty of finding it. First, you must choose one of several lanes; second, you must know at what point to watch for a track leading from that lane; third, you must know what to do when the track seems to be leading nowhere. On my first visit I was guided by a friend who possessed an *entrée*. After a long and muddy approach we sighted a thatched cottage in a wood. My immediate impression was: 'A dream cottage. But does it have water and a WC?' That question did not trouble Elgar. A woman who occupied Brinkwells during the 1960s gave a radio talk in which she said: 'I can't understand how Elgar put up with the inconvenience, because all they had were oil lamps and water which had to be pumped from miles away. No sanitation. Of course, Lady Elgar didn't like it, but he loved it . . . ' He did indeed, as is proven by his account of a typical day there: 'I rise about *seven* work till 8.15 – then dress, breakfast – pipe (I *smoke* again all day!) – then work till 12.30 lunch (pipe) – rest an hour – work till tea (pipe) – then work till 7.30 – change, dinner at 8. Bed at 10 – every day practically thus.' But it was not all tobacco and toil: 'We go lovely walks . . . woods are full of flowers . . . it really is lovely here – food good and plentiful – *much beer* . . . ' In another letter he announced: 'The woods are still carpeted with bluebells . . . there will be a full moon and all lovely and nightingales.' Such were the moments of delight which he transmuted into a sonata, a string quartet, a piano quartet, and part of a cello concerto. Lady Elgar noted that he was creating 'wonderful music, different from anything else of his'. As John Clare claimed that he found his poems in the fields, so Edward Elgar claimed that he found his music in the woods: 'The trees,' he told Jaeger, 'are singing my music – or have I sung theirs?' According to Sir Neville Cardus, 'Elgar maintained that in order to compose all a man needed to do was to "take it from the air" . . . '

Fine weather or foul, Brinkwells bore fruit throughout the year. Writing in September, Elgar told Lady Colvin (to whom, and to her husband, the Cello Concerto was dedicated): 'Here we have much bad weather, but the sunrises have been wonderful and quite make up for a lot of gales and rain: I have never seen anything so wonderful as the sun climbing over our view in the golden mist.' Next day, Lady Elgar's diary mentioned 'wonderful new music, real wood sounds and other lament . . . ' Michael Kennedy, author of a searching and sympathetic biography of Elgar, believed that this 'wonderful new music' was the start of the Cello Concerto, which he described as 'the music of wood smoke and autumn bonfires. . . ' Even at Brinkwells, however, the psychic wounds nagged, and age and the war took their toll. Michael Kennedy found that in the Cello Concerto 'sadness and disillusion are dominant and the music comes perilously close to what Jaeger would have called a "whine" of self-pity'.

On Armistice Day 1918 the Elgars returned to Brinkwells after a gloomy spell in London, where Lady Elgar underwent an operation. Once more Elgar divided his time between composition and country life. To Sir Sidney Colvin he wrote: 'I have commenced music again and hope to proceed: the axe however claims me and I make huge bonfires in the woods . . . ' Aware that Brinkwells had become a necessary ingredient of his own personal and professional life, Elgar tried to buy the cottage, and was bitterly disappointed when the owner, having agreed to sell, changed his mind. In 1920 Lady Elgar died, aged seventy-one. Elgar never wholly recovered from the loss, nor did he ever after compose great music. That he had already achieved greatness was due largely to his wife, who encouraged him during those years of poverty and neglect which he called 'The 30 (weary fighting) years of her help and devotion.' She was his shield against misfortune, and a balm to his temperament. 'All I have done was due to her,' he told Sir Walford Davies, 'and I am at present a sad and broken man – just stunned.' On a slip of paper he wrote the date of Lady Elgar's death, and under it Swinburne's lines:

> Let us go hence, my songs; she will not hear,
> Let us go hence, for singing-time is over,
> And over all old things, and all things dear.

After the funeral at Little Malvern, Elgar remained in Worcestershire for a month; then he returned to Brinkwells, where sorrow and solitude wore him down. He suffered fits of dizziness: 'I have had *three* more slight attacks and do not like the outlook at all . . . ' Then came a cry of despair: 'Music I loathe . . . it's all dead . . . The old life is over and everything seems blotted out.' Psychotherapy has its own definitions of depression. What one person accepts as mere discomfort, may to another seem agony. Nevertheless, we cannot avoid comparing Elgar's attitude with that of a greater composer who transcended a greater anguish with his Hammerklavier Sonata. As though to deepen the distress, Elgar learned that Brinkwells was about to be sold, and that many of the trees surrounding it had been felled: 'They have cut down the woods so much,' he complained, 'and made a road etc. which alters the look of the place . . . ' Although the trees were thinned, Brinkwells is still hidden among them, and photographs show that the cottage itself has not greatly altered since 1917. It is small, steeply thatched, and flanked by traces of a garden which in Elgar's day was tended by a villager. The garden house has vanished, but the thatch is in better condition than it was seventy years ago. Far below, the valley of the River Rother stretches away to a skyline of firs and sandy soil. The silence is pervasive. When Elgar lived there he may have quoted the words of his Sussex contemporary, Hilaire Belloc:

I will build a house with a deep thatch
To shelter me from the cold,
And there shall the Sussex songs be sung
And the story of Sussex told.

During the autumn of 1921 Elgar left Brinkwells for ever: 'to go,' as he put it, 'into the world as I did forty-three years ago – only I am disillusioned and old.' Reared as a Roman Catholic, he had long since rejected what he regarded as the childish fantasies with which religion tries to console mankind. Gerontius was awake at last, confronting facts which his dream could neither deny nor approve nor justify. Twenty years earlier, after the disastrous première of *Gerontius*, Elgar had told Jaeger: 'My heart . . . is now shut against every religious feeling and every soft, gentle impulse for ever,' On another occasion he declared: 'God is against art.' His unbelief was not founded solely on personal disappointment; it sprang from an awareness of Vergil's *lachrymae rerum*, the universal suffering which Matthew Arnold stated as a question:

And who can be *alone*, elate
While the world lies forlorn?

Writing to Laurence Binyon, Elgar arraigned 'the Heavenly Spirit which is cruelly obtuse to individual sorrow and sacrifice'. In another letter he cursed 'all-foolish providence'. In a third letter he cried out against the suffering of horses on the battlefield: 'I walk round and round this room cursing God for allowing dumb beasts to be tormented . . . ' During the last decade of his life he created an image or façade of himself as a race-going *bon viveur* whose moustache and bearing led some people to take him for a cavalry officer. Cecil Day Lewis made the point in a poem which compared the worldly old man with the younger composer of religious music; but Elgar had not quoted Swinburne lightly; his music-making was indeed over, except for a few pleasant pieces, such as the royal *Nursery Suite*.

After intense suffering, he died of cancer, refusing to see a priest. Elgar's daughter told Michael Kennedy that Elgar agreed to see a priest but was unconscious when the priest arrived. The priest told the daughter 'Your father has affirmed his faith.' In a letter to me, Michael Kennedy said: 'She went along with this statement because it let her off the hook about trying to get him buried in unconsecrated ground.' But his refusal had been anticipated by his Will, which stated that he wished to be buried, without any religious rite, at the confluence of his beloved Severn and Teme. In view of his remarks about God, the submission, if it ever occurred, seems less than convincing. Ernest Newman, who visited Elgar in hospital, said that the dying man made a statement, consisting of five words, which 'explains a good deal in him that has always been obscure or puzzling to us . . . It has a particular bearing, I am convinced, on that passion for public mystification of which the most remarkable expressions were his two 'enigmas' . . . ' Newman died without revealing Elgar's five words. They were, he said, 'too tragic for the ears of the mob'. Although the exact nature of Elgar's private enigma will almost certainly remain unknown, two facts are self-evident; first, he suffered a prolonged psychological conflict; second, in the light at Brinkwells he was able to see those radiant things which in the darkness he failed even to remember. That the visions were intermittent he himself acknowledged, by prefixing his Second Symphony with two lines from Shelley:

> Rarely, rarely, comest thou,
> Spirit of delight.

5
A Glimpse of Paradise: Brecknockshire

I have sometimes missed the way, but only once have I been lost. The experience was not wholly unpleasant. It occurred near Hay-on-Wye, in the ancient county of Brecknockshire, whence I intended to follow a steep lane over the mountains to Abergavenny in Monmouthshire; a day's march – twenty miles or so – that had been recommended to me by a Welsh friend who rated it among the finest routes in that part of Wales, which was indeed high praise, as anyone knows who has walked from Kilvert's Clyro to Landor's Llanthony, or from Trelleck to Penalt.

'Yes,' they had said at Hay, 'there is a mist this morning, but it will clear, I shouldn't wonder.'

I, on the other hand, did wonder, because Hay's narrow streets – when they did become briefly visible – looked remarkably like one another, and if I had not already explored them I would probably have passed the same bookshops several times. As it was, I managed to reach Cusop, which is just in Herefordshire, watered by Dulas Brook flowing from the Black Mountains, dividing England and Wales with a tumble of waterfalls. At Cusop the mist became so thick that I thought of returning to Hay, and would have done so had I not arranged to spend the night at Abergavenny. One day, perhaps, I shall make the journey again, or try to, for at present I still do not know precisely by what route I did make it. However, I remember climbing a lane, though the climb was perceptible only when my legs verified the gradient (an eighteenth-century Englishman said that Brecknockshire was aptly nicknamed 'Breakneckshire'). While climbing, I tried to imagine what was unfolding invisibly far below. 'It is Paradise,' my Welsh friend had assured me; and when I asked him to be more explicit he merely said: 'You will see for yourself.' But all I saw was a few yards of grey opacity. Had I shared Milton's piety, I might have uttered his prayer:

all mist from thence
Purge and dispense, that I may see and tell
Of things invisible to mortal sight.

Prayer or no prayer, the mist soon began to show rifts of visibility, lasting long enough to grant a glimpse of the Welshman's Paradise, for I was looking down on the tops of trees in a valley where one white farmhouse glistened like a snowdrop in the grass. Moment by moment, while the clarity increased, I saw that the far side of the valley soared to summits as high as the one on which I stood. I may never know where it was I did stand. Perhaps the glimpse was granted near Mardy, where Afon Honndu wanders through a combe, with Pen-y-Beacon in the background, more than two thousand feet high; or it may have been nearer to Hay, perhaps at Dan-y-Capel, on the edge of a great wood. No matter where it occurred, the vision was indeed of Paradise as my Welsh friend conceived it. The trees were hazily green; from the white farmhouse a plume of blue smoke spiralled like an Indian rope trick, the silence was heightened by hedges exuding sibilant mist; and over all stood the mountains.

Encouraged by the rifts, I decided to leave the lane and to follow one which seemed to lead in the right direction. I carried a map, of course, but not even the Ordnance Survey could mark every track; and it was then that I got lost, at the very instant when the tip of my nose was hit by a plump raindrop. Almost before I could zip up my jerkin, the first salvo straddled me, falling in straight lines that obliterated everything except the next few yards. There was no shelter nor any prospect thereof. By straying from the lane, I had reached a bald plateau sans tree or hedge or ditch or wall or barn. Already the rain was seeping under my collar. Soon it would reach the skin. I was at least a dozen miles from Abergavenny; probably more than a dozen. Then the track vanished, and when I went back, trying to rediscover it, I found two tracks, and could not remember which of them I ought to take. In the end I put back and rejoined the track that seemed to lead toward Abergavenny. Soaked literally to the skin, followed by a dog which knew that we were lost, I consoled myself with thoughts of a hot bath, dry clothes, and much food. After several monotonous miles – stumbling, peering, guessing – I sighted a tin hut, so I entered and took stock of my situation, checking first the time, which allowed another six or seven hours of daylight. Next, I removed the sodden jerkin and socks and boots, shaking some of the moisture from them. Finally, I sat on a bale of straw, more than ready for coffee and sandwiches. Unfortunately, the waitress at the hotel had not only omitted to pack the sandwiches; she had also failed to secure the cap of the thermos flask. From a dry corner of the haversack I rescued a slab of chocolate, sharing it with the dog; and from the bottom of the flask I drained a mouthful of tepid liquid. Never in all my travels had I suffered such an unpropitious journey. Halfway through the frugal meal, I noticed a bicycle under some sacks at the far end of the hut; and on the saddle stood a haversack, its flap unfolded to reveal a blue-and-white tea flask and a packet containing four beef sandwiches and a slice of cake. When I had eaten that unexpected feast, I placed on top of the haversack several silver coins equal to thrice the cost of what I had stolen. Do not ask – for I do not know – to whom the haversack belonged, nor whither the owner had gone. No doubt he was somewhere in that downpour, tending a lamb or mending a gate or carting a bale. I hope that he forgave my offence.

Outside again, the rain fell harder than ever, hissing when it hit the earth and bounced back from puddles. Even the dog seemed dispirited. Instead of ranging after rabbits, he kept close to heel, sometimes swerving to avoid the spray from my footsteps. Probably it was sheer luck, though I like to believe it was partly good navigation, that rescued me during the afternoon, when I heard a distant tractor. Descending toward the sound, I reached a lane, and guessed that it would lead to the main Abergavenny road. It did lead there, via Pandy, a small place with a wayside inn whose firelit windows winked warmly through the murk. Being too late and also too early to seek shelter there, I prepared myself for several miles of main road and cold rain. Fortunately, a woman happened to open the inn door while the dog was passing. 'Goodness gracious,' she cried, 'it is wet you look.' Pretending that her words referred to the dog's master, I called back: 'It is wet I am.'

Less than a minute later I was standing in front of a log fire, emitting pools of water on to the stone floor. Say what you will, the Welsh can be very likeable when they do not dislike you. The publican soon appeared, and the woman disappeared. After that, they exchanged roles, the woman appearing, the publican disappearing. Finally, they came together again, the woman with a cup of tea, the publican with a dry blanket.

'Just at present,' the woman confessed, 'we've not much to eat. Dai butcher doesn't call till teatime, and the Co-op hasn't called at all. Maybe the rain delayed him. However, if you would care for some ham and eggs and . . . ' she glanced at the publican, 'Ifor didn't have it all for dinner, so there's still some apple pie.'

While ham and eggs and Ifor's left-over were being prepared, I stripped off my clothes, wrapped myself in the blanket, and helped the publican to hang the garments above the fire. I forget how long I was there; it scarcely matters. The point is, a second blanket arrived, then bedroom slippers, then the meal, some more tea, and finally my clothes, which the publican and his wife had been toasting before the fire, so that everything felt more or less dry when I dressed again.

'There's luck for you,' the publican suddenly exclaimed. 'The rain has stopped. I wondered why everything seemed so quiet.' When he opened a window, we saw that the gutters were coping at last, the puddles were undimpled, and from the south came one of those blue rifts that I had seen during the morning.

'But there is no hurry,' the woman said. 'Finish your pipe first. Anyway,' she held up my boots, 'these are still steaming a bit.'

What a pleasant afternoon it became, and all so swiftly and unexpectedly. As we sat beside them, the logs were dimmed by the belated sunshine. Birds sang, and a pony and trap clip-clopped from Abergavenny market, laden with sheep-netting.

'During the war,' the publican was saying, 'in 1942 I think it was, fellows used to come here from London, bulging with five pound notes. And what do you think they wanted?'

'Antiques?' I suggested.

'Well,' he smiled, 'some of 'em did. Real villains they were. Knocking on cottage doors and offering the old people ten quid for dressers and chairs that were worth ten times as much. But most of 'em were after food, see? Black market stuff. They sold it to hotels. Made a fortune, some of 'em.'

'Tell him about . . . ' the woman began, then halted. 'No names, mind, but tell him.'

'Well,' said the publican, 'there was a farmer living not a hundred miles from Pandy, and he used to let the villains have butter and ham and the salmon he'd poached. All the things the rich will pay for. And by golly he did well out of it. We used to see him driving around in posh-looking . . . '

'No names,' the woman repeated.

'Quite right,' her husband agreed. 'But I'll tell you this much. They got him in the end. Had him up before the judge they did, and then into prison. Served him right, too.'

I reached Abergavenny in time to watch just such a sunset as had greeted Francis Kilvert when he, too, walked through this part of Wales: 'A lovely evening,' he wrote, 'and the Black Mountains lighted up grandly, all the furrows and water courses clear and brilliant. People coming home from market, birds singing, buds bursting, and the spring air full of beauty, life and hope.'

6
The Old Straight Road: Gloucestershire and Wiltshire

The grass track would have pleased Hazlitt, who exclaimed: 'Give me the clear blue sky over my head, and the green turf under my feet . . . I laugh, I run, I leap, I sing for joy.' Although I was not singing, I did feel the green turf under my feet, and a mild sense of adventure also, because I was following part of a Roman road, the Foss Way, which I had followed on horseback thirty years earlier, my task being to broadcast every evening for a fortnight, my task being to say something of the road and its makers and of my encounters thereon.

Now, after all those years, I parked the car near a wayside dell, called Jackaments Bottom, at a point where the modern road deviates from the old one, a few miles south of Cirencester. A spell of dry October weather had so hardened the turf that, in lieu of actually singing, I murmured Wordsworth's paean:

> 'tis joy enough and pride
> For one hour's perfect bliss, to tread the grass
> Of England . . .

Yet it was Rome, not England, that occupied my thoughts while I strolled at three miles an hour, flanked by flamboyant trees in an undulant countryside. Named after the ditch which runs beside it, the Foss Way spanned a large part of Roman Britain. Its northern terminus, Lincoln or *Lindum Colonia*, was a settlement of retired soldiers who received a grant of land nearby. Lincoln's Roman archway is the oldest still in use in Britain. Through it the Ninth Legion marched against the *Brigantes* in the north and against Queen Boudicca's *Iceni* in the east; but Lincoln was a southern as well as a northern terminus; from it led another Roman highway, Dere Street, northward to *Trimontium* near the Eildon Hills overlooking Sir Walter Scott's old home in Selkirkshire. Southward from Lincoln the modern road keeps close to the Foss Way and in places above it, offering a direct route from the Midlands to the south-west. Newark-on-Trent (whence the Roman canals and lesser roads reached the east coast); then to Leicester or Ratae (where a Roman mosaic is preserved in the basement of a shop); then Northleach in Oxfordshire (near the site of a Romano-British villa at Chedworth); Cirencester or *Corinium* (capital of a corn-growing region served by an inland harbour at Cricklade-on-Thames); and so to Bath, Axminster, and the Devon coast near Seaton.

I lingered awhile at Easton Grey, where the church (rebuilt in 1836 contains a memorial to a seventeenth-century couple, Arthur and Mary Ayde:

> Full of love, and free from discord here,
> Lived and died this very happy pair.
> When his wife pre-deceased him, the husband, being left alone,

Never ceased to sigh or ever ceased to moan
The loss of his dear comrade, dead and gone.

There are moments when sincerity transcends a merely literary criticism.

The River Avon enters Easton Grey, and the Romans forded it, for they were not as a rule bridge-builders, preferring to span wide rivers via rafts or boats lashed together. If the river was too wide to be bridged, they instituted a ferry, as across the Severn estuary and the Humber. If a sector of Celtic track suited their purpose, they co-opted it (the Foss shows an example of this near Radstock in Somerset). Rome gave to Britain a system of paved roads such as the natives had never seen before and would not see again until fourteen centuries had passed. Lacking either the will or the wit to emulate the Roman road-makers, the British failed even to maintain the road when Rome quit the country, so that ditches disintegrated, culverts became blocked, paving-stones were pilfered. As a result, letters from London to Perthshire travelled more quickly during the reign of the Emperor Hadrian than during the reign of George I.

Pedlars and packhorses carried a mixed cargo of merchandise, the most valuable exports being grain, gold, tin, jet, jewellery, quern stones, cloth (Roman merchants advertised *birrus Britannicus* or goat's wool as 'waterproof'), and two breeds of dog (a small hound for otter-hunting, and a larger one, rather like a boar-hound, as depicted on the Roman pavement at Cirencester). Villas and military posts near the Foss received imports of wine, marble, olive oil, silverware, and pine cones for use as altar fuel. Most of the soldiers were followers of Mithraism, an offshoot from the worship of Mazda, one of whose subordinates was Mithras, a spirit of Light. This cult symbolised the battle between Good and Evil, as recorded by Kipling's legionary:

Many roads thou hast fashioned; all of them lead to the light;
Mithras, also a soldier, teach us to die aright!

While riding down the Foss Way I discovered that the people living nearby called it The Old Straight Road and used it as a grapevine. Three miles south of Lincoln, for example, a woman called from her garden: 'At Keinton Mandeville tell my sister I've seen you. Keinton,' she added, 'is in Somerset.' Messages have passed along the Foss Way for almost two thousand years, and it is not merely fanciful to suppose that a Roman at Cirencester once said to a centurion: 'Tell Gaius the farrier that he's a grandfather. Mother and child are doing well. To hear him talk, you'd think the husband was the first man ever to have a son.' More important messages were either carried by couriers or signalled from military posts en route. In places far from a Roman road, murder and pillage occurred despite the long arm of imperial law, yet on the paved roads, patrolled by troops, a traveller passed safely. Law and order were the basis of *Romanitas*, the Roman legacy to European civilisation.

Rome, then, occupied my thoughts; but an Englishman cannot for long explore his own country without finding therein a sufficient source of contemplation. For example, Britain's premier river, the Thames, rises in a meadow not far from Jackaments Bottom. Some people have claimed that the true source lies near Cheltenham, but the Ordnance Survey agrees with John Leland, the Tudor antiquary, who said that the Isis or upper Thames 'riseth 3 myles from Cirencester, not far from a village called Kemble, within half a mile of the fosseway, where the very hed of Isis ys.' On most days of the year the source at Thames Head is as dry as the pile of stones which mark it; only after prolonged and heavy rain does the spring break to the surface, as it did during the 1960s, when some schoolboys paddled their canoe from the source to the Foss Way.

It is a strange experience, to follow this sector of the Way – a grass track, empty and neglected – and to know that it was once a major highway, more important because more communicative than any of our motorways. Having passed an airfield, the green road comes within a mile or so of Long Newton, where it is crossed by two lanes. Defoe remarked on the number of post-Roman roads which cross the Foss: 'We observ'd also how several crossroads . . . joyn'd it, tho' corruptly call'd also Foss, making the word Fosse as it were a common name for all roads.'

By choosing to walk on a Sunday, I gained a respite from the din of aircraft which day and night assail millions of Britons. In that quietude I continued for almost an hour, to a point where the Way was again crossed, this time by a lane to Shipton Moyne, the 'sheep farm' held by William de Mognye in 1221, and from 1325 until 1928 by the Estcourts, one of whom served as the parish priest from 1806 until 1856. Although Shipton Moyne lay out of sight, I remembered it as a hamlet of Cotswold stone, with a war memorial to eight of its inhabitants. Half a mile to the left stood Fosse Farm, and beyond it, after another straight mile, Upper Fosse Farm; and beyond that, after a few hundred yards, the Wiltshire border.

'The straight road,' said Edward Thomas, 'can only be made by those whose extreme haste and forethought have destroyed the power of joy . . . ' How true, as everyone knows who has driven on a motorway. The Roman colonisers, however, were not poets; they were soldiers and administrators, needing to get from A to B as quickly as possible. The course of Hadrian's Wall, switchbacking over the Northumbrian hills, illustrates the stamina with which the Roman road-builders kept to a straight line. If a swamp or some other natural obstacle did compel them to deviate, they made a short and sharp curve rather than a long and gradual one. The straightness of a Roman road seems all the more remarkable when you reflect that the builders possessed no mechanical direction-finder. The course of each road was plotted by soldiers holding wooden stakes 'dressed' in alignment. When a hill intervened, smoke signals may have been used to guide the surveyors.

By mid-morning, meanwhile, the sun was shining so warmly that I rested full-length on the turf, sipping coffee while the dog, a perennial optimist, chased elusive rabbits and absent foxes. Thus refreshed, I reached Easton Grey, one of the few hamlets which the Foss does enter. In 1242 the manor was held by Johannes Greiz, whose family came from Grays in Normandy. Today the hamlet lies off the beaten track, though in Roman times it was a thriving settlement. (The Georgian manor house has an inscribed sculpture: *Civilis fecit* or 'Civilis made me'.) The estate belonged either to a Roman or to a Briton whom we might now describe as a gentleman-farmer. Whatever his nationality, he occupied a house that must have aroused envy and awe among the natives who lived in primitive hovels. The Romans themselves designed their houses to suit the climate. In the south they needed shelter from the heat; in the north, shelter from the cold. The house at Easton Grey was probably modelled on a *villa rustica* or country residence, commodious but not stately. All such houses contained a courtyard, and nearly all were of one storey. Servants occupied a wing of the building, with their own hot baths. The walls of the principal rooms carried paintings; the floors were decorated with coloured mosaics or with tessellated pavements. Windows were fitted with glass panes (a luxury unknown to the early mediaeval Kings of England), and central heating came from hollow flue tiles above a basement hypocaust. Sanitation was more hygienic than in some British cottages today.

The Romans worshipped many gods and goddesses. As the mediaeval Church devised prayers for many aspects of life, so the Romans observed their own rites, with *Saturnalia* for sowing; *Robigalia* for the protection of crops; and *Consualia* for harvesting. Above all, the Romans venerated their home. When Cicero's house was destroyed by enemies, he stated a fact in the form of a question: 'Is there anything more closely hedged about with every kind of sanctity, than the individual home of each citizen?'

I walked two miles beyond Easton Grey, crossing a lane from Sherston to Malmesbury, at which point the Foss became a short stretch of metalled lane. At Lady's Wood Farm, knowing that the green track would soon become a lane again, I halted. Everything was very still; sometimes a robin sang, sometimes a sheep bleated, sometimes a leaf fell. When George Turner surveyed the district in 1794 he informed the Board of

Agriculture and Internal Improvement that the soil was rich: 'A loam,' he called it, 'intermixed with stones, on a subsoil of calcareous rubble or rock . . . producing great crops in a favourable time, but apt to burn and parch up in dry seasons . . . ' Rome valued the Cotswolds as a granary; England came to value them as a pasturage for sheep, the chief source of her mediaeval prosperity as an exporter of fleece and ultimately as a manufacturer of woollen garments, an achievement that is symbolised in the Woolsack on which the Lord Chancellor sits when he presides at the House of Lords.

Remembering my journey of thirty years ago, I looked ahead with an inward eye, following the Foss into Bath or *Aquae Sulis*, a city whose mineral waters were dedicated to *Sulis Minerva*; then westward to Keinton Mandeville, birthplace of John Henry Brodribb, whose stage name was Henry Irving; then to Ilchester, anciently an important town, containing a mint, a friary, a nunnery, and sixteen churches; then past Ashe House in Devon, home of Sir Winston Churchill, father of the first Duke of Marlborough, the victor at Ramillies, Malplaquet, and Blenheim; then through Axminster, whose first carpet is said to have been made in 1775 'by the pliant fingers of little children at Court House'; and finally to a footpath which might mark the course of the Foss as it reached the English Channel near Seaton. Then Roman soldiers who paved the last yard of the Way confirmed the truth of an old proverb: *Acti labores jocundi* or 'Missions completed are pleasant.'

My own mission, however, was only half completed. I had yet to return to the car, almost ten miles away, so, back I went, through Easton Grey, past Upper Fosse Farm, across a lane to Shipton Moyne, then across a stream, then across two other lanes, often halting to hear a robin, to quiz a tilth, or to prod my stick in the turf, wondering how deep the paved course lay. Excavations on the Foss in Somerset showed that it tallied with rules prescribed by Vitruvius, an eminent civil engineer; namely, a foundation of *stamen* or five inches of rubble; *rudus* or fifteen inches of coarse concrete; *nucleus* or ten inches of fine cement and local stone; and *pavium* or irregular paving stones in lime grouting.

As during the morning, my thoughts veered between modern England and imperial Rome. I tried to picture the early travellers on the Way, the soldiers, the administrators, the judges, the merchants, and the British peasants who stared wide-eyed at foreigners who took a daily bath, and built latrines and wrote poetry. Many of those peasants had shouted: 'Romans, go home!' When the Romans did go home, to defend their own city against barbarians, the British peasants shouted: 'Romans, come back!' But it was too late. Fighting among themselves, and refusing to unite against invasion, the British were pillaged and killed by more virile barbarians from Germany and Scandinavia. Writing in the depths of those Dark Ages, Bede painted a grim picture of the Britons' plight: 'The barbarians drive us into the sea and the sea drives us back to the barbarians.' Finding that the British would not defend themselves, the invaders reported that 'Britain is fertile, and the Britons are cowards.' In desperation the British bribed the invaders not to advance too far. Having accepted the bribe, the invaders anticipated the methods of modern trades unions, demanding an even bigger bribe. Sir Winston Churchill summed it up succinctly: 'Britain, reconciled to the Roman system, enjoyed in many respects the happiest, most comfortable, and the most enlightened time its inhabitants have had.'

At half past four the slight breeze died away and the few white clouds vanished. The weather forecast had been correct. Frost was imminent. Slowly the western sky turned as green as a duck's egg, and the first stars appeared, shimmering as if to confirm the cold. By the time I had reached Jackaments Bottom the trees were fading to a sombre russet. For almost nine hours I had walked, meeting no one, and hearing only an invisible cottager calling his dog. Even during the Roman occupation few people travelled after dark. They rose early, worked hard, and at night they sought the comfort and security of their own home; but the soldiers would have patrolled the Foss, and couriers would have ridden with urgent despatches. Looking back on the way I had come, I likened it to the Welsh section of a Roman road which A. G. Prys-Jones described:

Over the frosty moorland
The moon is rising high,
And out of the wintry silence
The wraiths of Rome ride by.

7
Gathering of the Clans: Perthshire and Aberdeenshire

For more than thirty miles the road from Blairgowrie to Braemar enters nothing which a southron would rate as a village. Blairgowrie itself is a spruce little town, crowded during the summer, but at other times restful. Local horticulturalists ply a brisk trade in raspberries and strawberries.

North of Blairgowrie the route follows the course of a road that was built by Viscount Bury's regiment, chiefly as a result of the Jacobite Rebellion in 1715, when the English army had been hindered and endangered by lack of adequate highways. In 1724 Lord Lovat suggested to King George I that a series of metalled roads might curb the unruly Highlanders by reducing the isolation which enabled them to live a semi-autonomous existence. Dr. Johnson stated the problem succinctly: 'Mountainous regions are sometimes so remote from the seat of government, and so difficult of access, that they are very little under the influence of sovereigns, or within the reach of national justice.' The King having approved Lord Lovat's suggestion, General Wade undertook a survey of the Highlands, which confirmed his own belief that a network of roads would indeed help the army to suppress an insurrection by the clans. Within a few months his soldiers had completed seven miles of road between Fort William and Fort Augustus. During the next six years they built nearly two hundred and forty miles of road, through the highest and wildest terrain in Britain. 'Wade's roads', as they were called, did much to civilise the life of the Highlands. The road between Blairgowrie and Braemar, a distance of thirty-four miles, was completed in 1750 by one hundred men from Viscount Bury's regiment.

Beyond Blairgowrie the road crosses the River Ericht at the Bridge of Cally, overlooking the river's upper reaches, which are known as Black Water. Eastward looms the Forest of Alwyth, fifteen hundred feet above sea level. A few cottages and hotels stand beside the road, lonely as milestones that have been set too far apart. After a dozen miles the road sends a lane downhill to a *clachan* or cluster of cottages which the map calls Millton. On the first of my journeys I passed that lane; on the second I followed it and was rewarded by reaching an oasis in a desert of rock. I spent an hour there, resting beside a stream while June sunlight polished the snow-capped summits. No one came, no one went; which disappointed me because I wished to learn something about the *clachan*. Its name and its river suggested that the place had been built beside a watermill.

Rejoining the Braemar road on higher ground, I felt the wind again – the Highlands' perennial voice – and saw the bald pate of Mount Blair, 2,441 feet in the sunshine. The road soon began a gradual descent to the Spittal of Glenshee, sometimes known as the Fairy Glen, which contains two hotels and not much else, all dominated by snow-streaked mountains. The Spittal or hospital was founded by the mediaeval Church as a haven for travellers crossing the hazardous Mounth range. One of those travellers was King Robert II of Scotland, who lodged at the hospice on 27th June 1376. The building itself vanished long ago. At Glenshee a track reaches Dalmunzie House Hotel, nearly a mile into the glen, one of the most agreeably isolated hotels in Britain. When I stayed there during summer the last of the sunset was so soon succeeded by the first of the sunrise that I marvelled to hear the cuckoos producing such sounds from so little sleep. At three o'clock in the morning they were as clamorous as Respighi's *The Birds*. On both sides of the glen the mountains rise like green cliffs, and the middle of the valley resembles a vast golf course, watered by streams. The scene was praised by an anonymous poet four centuries ago:

> Glen Shee, the vale that close beside me lies,
> There sweetest sounds are heard of deer and elk . . .
> Below the great Ben Gulabin's grassy height
> Of fairest knolls that lie beneath the sun
> The valley climbs.

Ben Gulabin is indeed a grassy height, somewhat loftier than its neighbour, Creagan Bheithe, each exceeding 2,500 feet. *The Book of the Dean of Lismore* mentions a hunter, Diarmid Mac O'duine, who climbed Ben Gulabin in order to kill a dangerous wild boar:

> The great old boar, him so well known in Shee,
> The greatest in the wild boar's haunts e'er seen.

Among the various Gaelic words for 'mountain' are Ben, Beinn, Creag, Monadh, Sgurr, Stob, Strone. It was this blend of bare mountains and wooded glens that prompted Sir Walter Scott to say: 'Perthshire forms the fairest portion of the northern kingdom.'

Having already covered twenty mountainous miles from Blairgowrie, a stranger may suppose that the next fifteen miles must be a come-down, aesthetically as well as physically; but this is not so, because Braemar and the Spittal of Glenshee stand at almost the same altitude, and the road between them is the steepest and most spectacular section of the entire journey, starting at Glenshee itself, where the road turns sharply from west-north-west to north-north-east, crossing a small bridge over the upper reaches of Black Water, which at that point is called Shee Water. Now the road twists and climbs to the Devil's Elbow, a hairpin bend on a 1-in-6 gradient at a height of almost two thousand feet. Since I first drove along it, at twelve cautious miles an hour, the bend has been 'improved' for the benefit of motorists who wish not to see the surrounding countryside.

Next comes a pass which the maps call Cairnwell, though its correct name is Cairnwall. This must be the highest, or almost the highest, road in Britain, topped by Glas Maol, whose summit marks the boundary between Angus, Perthshire, and Aberdeenshire. In 1947 The Mount was so thickly covered by snow that Seton Gordon likened it to the ice-caps of Iceland and Spitsbergen. The prospect hereabouts appalled Defoe: 'This frightful country,' he wrote, 'all one undistinguish'd range of mountains and woods, overspread with vast and almost uninhabited rocks . . . ' Fashion has indeed changed, for modern tourists no longer share the Augustan dread of wild scenery; like Wordsworth, they prefer

> To roam at large among the unpeopled glens
> And mountainous retirement, only trod
> By devious footsteps.

Soon the road enters Aberdeenshire, the land of Forbes and of Gordon. The Forbes established themselves of the Braes of Forbes seven hundred years ago; their chief is Scotland's premier Baron, and their tartan was designed in 1822, using the dark green of the Forty-second Highland Regiment, superimposed with thin white stripes. The Gordons were a twelfth-century Berwickshire family who in 1449 became Earls of Huntly; their chief is the Marquis of Huntly, and their dark green tartan was adopted by the Gordon Highlanders, with the addition of thin yellow stripes. People who care for such things may wish to know that a Highland gentleman's full dress consisted of a feile-beag or kilt; a waistcoat of scarlet, or white, or tartan; low-cut shoes; silver-mounted sporran with a brooch to fasten the plaid; a waist-belt, a baldric or sword-belt, a claymore or broadsword, a dirk, a pair of pistols, a powder-horn, and a broad bonnet with badge or crest.

The Scottish clans have no precise equivalent anywhere else in the world, being more intimate and at the same time wider-ranging than the tribal system. Although the chiefs have lost much of their former power and mystique, the clan is by no means an anachronism. The chiefs are still visited and consulted by people of Scottish descent, some of whom live in distant parts and have never before stood on Scottish soil. The chieftainship of a clan is basically hereditary and may pass to a woman; in certain circumstances, the chief may choose a successor from his own relatives. Until the middle of the eighteenth century, a Highland chief resembled the one in Aytoun's poem:

> He kept his castle in the north,
> Hard by the thundering Spey;
> And a thousand vassals dwelt around,
> All of his kindred they.

Scott's *Waverley* showed the chief as a warrior: 'He crowded his estates with tenantry, hardy indeed, and fit for the purposes of war, but greatly outnumbering what the soil was calculated to maintain. These consisted chiefly of his own clan, not one of whom he suffered to quit his lands if he could possibly prevent it.' Scott mentioned a chief who enlisted any suitable vassals on condition that they assumed his name, MacIvor. Gilbert White, on the other hand, warned his fellow-Englishmen to be on their guard against 'the wild natives, their superstition, their prejudices, their sordid ways of life . . . ' Defoe, however, admired the Highland lairds 'who appear at court, and in our camps and armies, as polite and as finish'd gentlemen as any from other countries, or even among our own.'

On the Aberdeenshire sector of this road, the mediaeval Church built a second hospice for travellers, called Shean

Spittal, at a point where the mountains lose something of their greenness and appear even more desolate while the road makes yet another long and sinuous descent, followed on the right by the Water of Clunie. Presently the landscape becomes softer, the soil more fertile, the sheep more numerous. Three miles short of Braemar, the military route leaves the modern one, crossing Fraser's Bridge, a pleasant detour into Braemar.

Dominated by Cairn Toul (4,241 feet), Braemar stands on both sides of the Water of Clunie. The western side is called Auchendryne or 'field of thorns'; the eastern side is called Castledon, after King Malcolm Canmore's castle, fragments of which are still visible. Seton Gordon, who seldom made a mistake when writing of the Highlands, did err in saying that Tomintoul 'shares with Braemar the doubtful honour of being the highest village in Scotland'. Braemar is thirty feet lower than Tomintoul and both are lower than the Lowland village of Wanlockhead (1,380 feet). Nevertheless, the altitude and latitude ensures that Braemar is a cold place, especially during January and February (in 1895 the temperature fell to minus seventeen degrees F.). Since Braemar in summer is crammed with tourists, I prefer to arrive during early May, or in late October, when the villagers are in every sense at home.

The sixth Earl of Mar raised the Old Pretender's standard in what is now the Invercauld Arms Hotel at Braemar, a granite mansion, much changed since it was built two centuries ago. The views, however, have not greatly changed since Thomas Pennant stayed there as the guest of the Farquharsons, soon after the house had been built: 'Nothing,' he wrote, 'can be more beautiful than the different views from the several parts of it.' Northward a line of 'immense ragged and broken crags bound one side of the prospect . . . ' Southward the mountains form 'a vast theatre, the bosom of which is covered with extensive forests of pine . . . ' Pennant exaggerated when he said that many of the peaks were 'topped with perpetual snow'. Snow falls at Braemar on about sixty days each year, but Cairn Toul never stays snowy all the time. Pennant noted that the Braemar landowners paid half a crown to anyone who caught an eagle (about seventy birds were trapped between 1776 and

1786). Sixty years later the district contained ospreys, goshawks, ravens, Montagu's harriers, falcons, martens, pole-cats, and wildcats.

If you ask the villagers the way to Invercauld Chest they will point to a rock that was so-named because the Invercauld charters were hidden there during the 1715 rebellion, when the raising of the Jacobite standard evoked a resonant defiance:

> The standard on the Braes o'Mar
> Is up and streaming rarely;
> The gathering pipes on Lochnagar
> Are sounding long and early.

Braemar Castle, north of the village, belongs to the Farquharsons of Invercauld. Set on a hillock beside the Dee, it was built by the second Earl of Mar in 1628. Fifty years later the Jacobites attacked and severely damaged it; and fifty years after that the damage was repaired. Pennant described the castle as 'a square tower, the seat of the ancient Earls of Mar; in later times a garrison to curb the discontented chieftains; but at present unnecessarily occupied by a company of Foot being rented by the Government from Mr. Farquharson of Invercauld . . . ' Further north, Lochnagar, a granite-based mountain, impressed Lord Byron:

> Oh for the crags that are wild and majestic,
> The steep frowning glories of dark Lochnagar!

Byron attended Aberdeen Grammar School before proceeding to Harrow. As a child of ten he was summoned to the headmaster's study, to be told that he had succeeded his great-uncle as Lord Byron. Afterwards, when his name at roll-call received the prefix *Dominus*, the child was so moved that he wept and could not reply 'Adsum'.

Under the lee of Lochnagar stands the Gaelic *Bouchmorale* or 'stately home' known nowadays as Balmoral Castle. An earlier castle on the site had belonged to the Gordons and then to the Farquharsons who in 1745 were heavily fined for their

Jacobite activities, and in 1798 they sold Balmoral to the Earl of Fife. In 1852 the castle was partly demolished to make way for a larger one which Queen Victoria called 'A pretty little Castle in the old Scotch style'. In 1852 the castle was bought by the Queen and Prince Albert, who demolished it and built the present stately residence. From Balmoral the Royal Family travel a few miles to attend an event that has made Braemar famous throughout the world, the Highland Gathering or Games. Athletics had been held at Braemar during the Middle Ages, notably when King Malcolm Canmore summoned the clans to the Braes of Mar, there to select the fittest men for his bodyguard. The modern Games have their roots in the Braemar Wrights' Society, founded in 1817 as an association of workmen who paid fourpence a year as insurance against hard times. In 1826 the association became the Braemar Highland Society, and it still provides for widows, orphans, and sick or elderly members. Organised games were held at Braemar in 1832, but they did not attract wide notice until 1848, when Queen Victoria watched them and agreed to become their patron, whereafter the Society styled itself 'Royal'. In 1906 the Queen's son-in-law, the Duke of Fife, gave the Society a twelve-acre site, with accommodation for thirty thousand spectators.

I have met two successive honorary secretaries of the Gathering, both of whom assured me that while the Games are taking place not a bed can be had within thirty miles of Braemar. Athletes and spectators arrive from many parts of the world. There are running races, throwing the weight, tossing the caber, tug-of-war, a sword dance for local children under nine years old, and a Gaelic dance, *sean truibbas*. Sartorial decorum is compulsory and precise: 'All competitors,' says the programme, 'must be dressed in Highland Costume, except for Running and Jumping Competitions, in which they must compete in University Running Dress. This Rule will be strictly enforced.' At noon the massed pipe bands march round the arena, uttering a skirl that has for centuries accompanied the Highlanders in war and in peace, in joy and in sorrow, in life and in death. The bagpipe seems to have been introduced by the Romans, who had probably heard the Egyptian drone-pipe. According to Dr. Percy Scholes, 'The key of the Highland pipe is that of A major with a natural G and with the C and F something between sharp and the natural – a unique scale, but with some similarities to the Near East'. Not everyone enjoys the sound of a bagpipe. Shakespeare and Francis Kilvert said some very harsh things about it. Nevertheless, the instrument was common throughout much of mediaeval England, and the Duke of Northumberland retains his own piper at Alnwick Castle. The music or *pibroch* may be a lament, a challenge, a march, a welcome, a salute, or a song for the chief's boat, as in *The Lady of the Lake*:

> Proudly our pibroch has thrilled to Glen Fruin,
> And Bannocher's groans to our slogan replied;
> Glen Luss and Ros-dhu, they are smoking in ruin,
> And the best of Loch Lomond lie dead on her side.

When the present Sovereign, Queen Elizabeth II, attends the Highland Gathering she finds a more peaceable scene and a more cordial reception, for she is descended from King James VI of Scotland, and her maternal grandfather was a Scottish peer. To daughter and mother, therefore, the Highlanders at Braemar extend a Gaelic *Cead Mille Failte* or 'A Hundred Thousand Welcomes'.

8
After the Storm: Dorset

When touched by sunlight, the summit of Golden Cap illuminates its own name. Near Eype, however, the West Cliff glows yellow; and at Burton Bradstock the rocks are tawny. It was from high ground thereabouts that John Gay saw the road ahead:

> Through Bridport's stony lanes our route we take,
> And the proud steep descent to Morcomb Lake.

Another lofty scene, Charmouth Down, was described by John Hutchins as 'ye Plinlimon of Dorsetshire'. At Lulworth the cliffs are so steep that a thankful parent erected a notice: 'This marks the spot whereon E.H.L., aged 11 years, Fell from the summit of the cliffs, a descent of 380 feet, September 7th

1892. She miraculously escaped without sustaining lifelong injury. S.T.S.L.'

You will look in vain for any fishing fleet off the Dorset coast. Only a few small craft now work there. Defoe, by contrast, sighted many Bridport boats whose catch of mackerel 'proved to be an incredible number, insomuch, that the men could hardly draw them to shore . . . such was the plenty of fish that year, that mackerell, the finest and largest I ever saw, were sold at the sea side a hundred for a penny'. Since Defoe sometimes spoke harshly about countryfolk, it is pleasant to repeat his praise of Dorset society: 'A general freedom of conversation, agreeable, mannerly, and kind, and good runs thro' the whole body of the gentry . . . mix'd with the best of behaviour . . . such as I nowhere see better in all my observations thro' the whole isle of Britain.'

The Dorset coast has witnessed many wrecks, notably that of the *Earl of Abergavenny*, commanded by John Wordsworth, the poet's brother, which drifted on to rocks near Portland, not through her Captain's negligence, but because of an incompetent pilot, to whom the unfortunate Wordsworth cried: 'Pilot, you have ruined me!' Most of the passengers and crew perished. William and Dorothy Wordsworth were overwhelmed by grief. The sister wrote: 'I can never again have a *perfect* – that is, unchastized joy in this world.' The brother prayed: 'God keep the rest of us together. The set is now broken.' For two months he was unable to write. Thereafter he unburdened himself:

> Not for a moment could I now behold
> The smiling sea, and be what I have been.
> The feeling of my loss with ne'er be told;
> This, which I know, I speak with mind serene.

A mile or two inland from Burton Bradstock stands the village of Shipton Gorge, formerly a *scipetune* or 'sheep farm', though never a gorge, because the place was named after a thirteenth-century lord of the manor, Thomas Gorges, who came from Gorge in Coutance. Shipton's modern houses bestride a hill; the old settlement lies lower down, where the period houses compose an attractive cluster. From Shipton a footpath leads to an earthwork with views of the sea and two landmarks, Lewesdon Hill and Pilsdon Pen, each about nine hundred feet high, of which it used to be said: 'As much akin as Lew'son Hill and Pilsdon Pen' . . . a misleading comparison, for whereas Lewesdon is rounded and wooden, Pilsdon is elongated and bare, crowned by an Iron Age fort whose summit in clear weather overlooks Glastonbury Tor (twenty-seven miles away), the Blackdown Hills (forty miles away), and the Quantock Hills (forty-three miles away). When the Wordsworths were living at Racedown, the Dorset contours reminded Dorothy of Westmorland: 'We have hills which, seen from a distance, can almost take the character of mountains . . . ' The summit of Pilsdon, she noted, was in a 'wild state, covered with furze and broom. These delight me as they remind me of our native wilds . . . ' The district was portrayed in *Leweson Hill*, one of those long topographical poems which became popular during the eighteenth century. Its author, William Crowe, served as rector of Stoke Abbot and as Public Orator at the University of Oxford. Lewesdon Hill dominates Marshwood Vale and a posy of rustic place-names: Duckpool, Fishpond, Cutty Stubbs, Shaves Cross, Plenty House, Pomice Farm, Whitchurch Canonicorum. Crowe himself was in two minds about the Vale, calling it

> Cold, vapourish, miry, wet, and to the flocks
> Unfriendly, when autumnal rains begin
> To drench the spungy turf . . .

During spring and summer he took a kindlier view:

> There woods, there blooming orchards, there are seen
> Herds ranging, or at rest beneath the shade
> Of some wide-branching oak; there goodly fields
> Of corn, and verdant pasture, thence the kine
> Returning with their milky treasure home
> Store the rich dairy; such fair plenty fills
> The pleasant vale of Marshwood . . .

Pleasant indeed; and pleasant, too, a brook at the foot of the hill, which, as in Crowe's day,

> flows along
> Untainted by the commerce of the world.

Crowe wrote lovingly and from close observation. Like Gilbert White's verse vignettes, his best lines justify the verdict of Washington Irving, an American who spent several years in England; 'The pastoral poets of other countries appear as if they had paid nature an occasional visit and have become acquainted with her general charm; but the British poets have lived and revelled with her – they have wooed her in her most secret haunts – they have watched her minutest caprices.'

From the high ground between Lewesdon and Shipton Gorge you look down at Berwick Farm, set close to the sea and therefore to the storms, one of which ended so auspiciously that, if the story were told as fiction, it would sound too good to be true. The drama began on a wild January day in 1506, when a ship ran for shelter in Weymouth harbour. On board were Philip, Archduke of Austria, and his wife Joanna, who had inherited the kingdom of Castile from her mother, Queen Isabella, Already King *de jure uxoris*, Philip was sailing from Middleburgh in order to assert his sovereignty *de facto*. One account suggests that the royal couple intended to visit England, and that King Henry VII sent Lord Arundel with three hundred horsemen to receive them; but the manner of their arrival suggests that the visit was caused solely by the storm. The point is, this unexpected arrival of a foreign vessel caused alarm because relations between England and some of her continental neighbours were tetchy, and neither the Archduke nor his wife could speak English. The Weymouth townsfolk therefore informed the High Sheriff of Dorset, Sir Thomas Trenchard, who lived at Wolfeton Manor near Dorchester. Having sent a horseman to inform the King at Windsor, Sir Thomas rode immediately to Weymouth. On confirming the royal visitors' identity, he invited them to become his guests at Wolfeton. The party thereupon proceeded to a mansion which Thomas Hardy mentioned in *A Group of Noble Dames*: 'Going out of Casterbridge by the low-lying road which eventually conducts to Ivell, you see on the right hand an ivied manor-house, flanked by battlemented towers, and more than distinguished by the size of its many windows. Though still of good capacity, the building is much reduced from its original grand proportions . . . ' Following his custom of either inventing or distorting proper names, Hardy introduced the Trenchards by stating that Wolfeton 'was formerly the seat of the ancient and knightly family of Drenghards . . . '

Meanwhile, since Sir Thomas could not converse with his guests, he felt the need of an interpreter who might join them as a suitable member of the party. Fortunately, one of his own young kinsmen not only spoke Spanish but also lived nearby and seemed in every way worthy to sit above the salt. This kinsman was John Russell of Swyre, a parish near Shipton Gorge. Known locally as 'Farmer' Russell, he occupied Berwick Farm (Old English *berewic* or 'corn farm'), which still stands, modernised and enlarged, overlooking a secluded lane that runs parallel with the River Brede. Like many other lanes in the district, this one seldom attracts tourists. Even during the summer I have driven from Shipton Gorge to the outskirts of Dorchester, on lanes which passed only a few cottages, and carried only a fieldward tractor or a farmwife driving to the shops. Once you have left the main roads, you enter a Dorset which William Barnes would recognise as his own county of cattle and sheep,

> An' hearty folk to laugh and zing,
> An' parish-churches in a string,
> An' tow'rs o' merry bells to ring,
> An' white roads up athirt the hills.

The Russells – who may have been named after one of their red-headed French ancestors (*roussel* or 'red') – had lived in Dorset since the Middle Ages, as lords of Kingston Russell, the *Cyninges-tun* or 'King's manor', which, during the reign of

Edward I, was held in return for counting the pieces on the King's chessboard and ensuring that they were replaced after each game. A later Russell, a Gascon wine merchant, settled at Weymouth, founding a business which enabled 'Farmer Russell' to travel on the Continent. When the Russells of Kingston Russell became extinct, the other branch continued to hold the small estate at Berwick. Thither, then, rode the High Sheriff's servant, summoning John Russell to Wolfeton. Despite his rustic soubriquet, John was well-mannered and well-read. His arrival certainly pleased the royal guests, partly because he spoke their own language, and partly because he proved to be a charming companion. After a few days the King's reply reached Wolfeton, inviting the guests to Windsor Castle. One would like to know John Russell's feelings when, instead of returning to Berwick, he was asked to escort the royal couple to Windsor. However, we do know that he impressed the English King as favourably as he had impressed the Castilian, because the latter introduced him to the former as 'a man fit to stand before Princes'. Russell, in short, had arrived at the right place, at the right time, with the right qualifications; for Henry VII, a usurper, needed men of the middling sort, well-bred and industrious, but not connected with a powerful aristocratic clique. Himself of Welsh ancestry, Henry had already promoted the Welsh Sitsyllts, who having anglicised themselves as Cecil, received a peerage. The King, at all events, judged Russell to be worthy of advancement. Within a short time the erstwhile farmer was invited to serve at Court. He agreed, and ultimately became a Gentleman of the Privy Chamber. All seemed set fair until, after only three years, Henry died; but by that time Russell had established himself so securely that he went with the new King, Henry VIII, on the first of several campaigns against France, where he distinguished himself in battle and was created Knight Banneret. Not long afterwards he accompanied Henry to the Field of the Cloth of Gold, a pageant of jousting and feasting wherewith Wolsey tried to ease the tension between England and France. When the tension increased, Sir John Russell served with a naval expedition against Brittany. For several years he undertook diplomatic missions in France and Italy, sometimes playing a cloak-and-dagger role. According to Lord Herbert of Cherbury, he persuaded the Duke of Bourbon to desert the French King; Russell, said Cherbury, 'in disguised habit often treated with him (as I find by records) and made him finally revolt'. In 1539 Russell was created Baron Russell. Ten years later he became Earl of Bedford.

His career was spectacular and profitable. By marrying the widow of Sir Guy Sapcote he acquired an estate at Chenies in Buckinghamshire, from which he took his baronial title. During the dissolution of the monasteries he received abbeys at Woburn in Bedfordshire, at Tavistock in Devonshire, and at Thorney in Cambridgeshire, together with manors on Exmoor and a sizeable estate in what became Covent Garden and the Strand. At the beginning of the sixteenth century John Russell had been an obscure country gentleman; by the middle of the century he was a member – in a sense the founder – of a family that was included among Paul Heintzer's list of 'The Illustrious Families of England'. Unlike some other 'new men', Russell nurtured his rural roots; indeed, he extended them when, as Lord Lieutenant of Dorset and of Devon and of Cornwall, he not only maintained Berwick Farm but also bought Kingston Russell, which once again became a home for his relatives. The present Kingston Russell House, built during the seventeenth and eighteenth centuries, and enlarged in 1913, was the birthplace of Nelson's friend, Captain Thomas Masterton Hardy; in the same house died John Lothrop Motley, author of *The Rise of the Dutch Republic*; another occupant was an army officer of the 1914 war, Julian Gribble, VC, who died of wounds on the day the war ended. Thomas Hardy mentioned Kingston Russell House in *Desperate Remedies*, calling it Knapwater House and assessing it through the eyes of an architect: 'The house was regularly and substantially built of clean grey freestone throughout, in that plainer fashion of Greek classicism which prevailed at the latter end of the last century, when the copyists called designers had grown weary of fantastic variations in the Roman orders. The main block approximated to a square on the ground plan, having a projection in the centre of each side, surmounted by a pediment.'

At a time when many courtiers were plotting against one another and also against the Crown, John Russell might, like Warren Hastings, have been amazed by his own moderation. Sir Thomas Wyatt, a traitor whom Russell had indicted, saluted him as an honest man; the Spanish diplomats, those masters of deception, paid tribute to his integrity; and when Wolsey fell from favour, Russell remained his friend despite the danger of such loyalty. Loyalty, in fact, was the foundation of Russell's success. While others rose and fell with one Sovereign, he retained the trust of five Sovereigns. He died at a good age, in his house beside the Strand. His descendants, who became Dukes of Bedford, still own some of the estates which 'Farmer' Russell acquired.

9
A West-of-Wessex Girl: Cornwall

Saint Juliot lies a few miles inland from Boscastle on the north coast of Cornwall. It is a parish without a village. Although Thomas Hardy described such seclusion as 'a little one-eyed, blinking sort o' place', his own experiences at Saint Juliot were so memorable that he regarded them as the key to much of his life. When he was young he wrote a novel about them; when he was old, a sequence of poems. Like Saint Juliot itself, those writings are tinged with Atlantic spray, and the best approach to them is via Boscastle, a miniature harbour, one of the very few on the north Cornish coast, and probably the most difficult to enter.

Five centuries ago Boscastle was visited by John Leland, chaplain and itinerant antiquary to King Henry VIII, who called the village 'Botreaux Castelle vulgo Boscastle . . . the

Lorde Bottreux was Lord of this Toun, a man of old Cornish lineage . . . ' In 1302 the manor belonged to William de Botreus, whose family probably came from Les Bottereux in Normandy. Leland formed a low opinion of Boscastle ('a very filthy Toun, il kept'), yet he fulfilled his task as topographer, explaining that 'the Toune of Boscastle lyith upon the Brow of a rokky Hill . . . and so goith down by length to the Northe toward the se . . . There is a church in it, as I remembre, of S. Simpherian'. Today there is no church; worshippers must attend Saint Marthiana's at Minster, about a mile inland.

From Boscastle a narrow lane passes Saint Knuet's church at Lesneweth, (Celtic *lis* or 'palace' and *newydh* or 'new') another parish without a village, formerly the seat of a local chief. Climbing among woods and streams, the lane enters a district whose place-names are of farms rather than of villages: Penpol Helset, Gunvillick, Tregrylls, Trevilla, Trewannion. Some of the hills exceed a thousand feet, topped with prehistoric tumuli. On none of six journeys have I ever met a vehicle in this lane, though I did once see a stationary car near Saint Juliot church. After a steep descent and a sharp left-hand turn, the lane climbs through more woods and eventually reaches the few scattered cottages and farms which comprise Saint Juliot. Lying some way below the lane, the church of Saint Juliotta recalls the piety of parishioners whose numbers have dwindled since machinery ousted men and women from their work on the land. Many other country churches are more impressive than Saint Juliotta's, but few are so undisturbed by passing travellers, and fewer still are so intimately associated with a great writer.

The association began when Hardy, son of a Dorset stonemason, was twenty-nine years old, apprenticed to a Dorchester architect. His published writings consisted of one article in *Chambers Journal*, entitled 'How I Built Myself a House'. Nevertheless he still hoped to become an author; in fact, he was staying with his parents near Dorchester, rewriting his first novel, *The Poor Man and the Lady*, which had been rejected by two publishers. In February 1870 the rewriting was interrupted by a letter from Hardy's employer, requiring him to visit Cornwall, 'to take a plan and particulars of a church I am about to rebuild there'. A week later the young architect went by train to Launceston whence he was driven to Saint Juliot, a journey of some eighteen miles across lonely country. At that point the story was continued by his diary: 'March 7. The dreary yet poetical drive over the hills. Arrived at St. Juliot Rectory between 6 and 7. Received by a young lady in brown. . . ' There the story was resumed by the young lady herself, Emma Lavinia Gifford, the rector's sister-in-law, who wrote: 'The front door bell rang and the architect was ushered in. I had to receive him alone . . . I was immediately arrested by his familiar appearance, as if I had seen him in a dream – his slightly different accent, his soft voice; I noticed a blue paper sticking out of his pocket . . . I thought him much older than he was. He had a beard and a rather shabby greatcoat . . . Afterwards he seemed younger, and by daylight especially so . . . The blue paper proved to be the MS. of a poem, and not a plan of the church, he informed me, to my surprise.'

Hardy's diary for the following day made no reference to Miss Gifford, but it did mention the church: 'Staying there and drawing and measuring all day, with intervals for meals at the rectory.' Two days later, however, Miss Gifford was again mentioned, this time under her initials: 'Went with E.L.G. to Beeny Cliff. She on horseback . . . ' Already the lady was being feminine, for on that same afternoon, having lost two of her initials, she paid little attention to the architect: 'E. provokingly reading as she walked . . . ' But the fire had been kindled, and the lady recorded the fact, in a memoir written long afterwards: 'My Architect came two or three times a year from that time to visit me. I rode my pretty mare Fanny and he walked by my side, and I showed him some more of the neighbourhood – the cliffs, along the roads, and through the scattered hamlets . . . We sketched and talked of books; often we walked to Boscastle Harbour . . . ' Many years later, when he had resurrected the ancient kingdom of Wessex as the scene of his novels, Hardy remembered Emma's knowledge of north Cornwall; she was, he said, 'My West-of-Wessex girl'. During one of those early excursions, while the couple were having a picnic, Hardy accidentally dropped a drinking glass in the stream. The incident must have imprinted itself on Emma's memory, because she recorded it in her memoir: 'We once lost a tiny picnic-tumbler, and there it is to this day no doubt between the two boulders.'

Meanwhile, having inspected the church, Hardy decided that parts of it were beyond repair and must be demolished. This grieved him because he did not approve of the so-called restoration which had marred many other churches. Fortunately, he drew several sketches before the demolition began (a facsimile of one of them hangs on the west wall). Having done his work at Saint Juliot, and having fallen in love with Emma, Hardy returned to Dorset and soon finished his novel, sending it in batches to Emma, who made a fair copy for the printer. Renamed *Desperate Remedies*, the book appeared in 1871. It was poor stuff from a man in his thirty-first year. Relying overmuch on coincidence, the plot foreshadowed Hardy's belief that the *primum mobile* of every event is a blend of Chance and of a Power which knowingly torments its own creation. His second novel *Under the Greenwood Tree*, showed achievement as well as promise. In a letter submitting the book to Macmillan, Hardy wrote: 'I have sent by railway the manuscript of a tale called Under the Greenwood Tree. It is entirely a story of rural life, and attempts have been made to draw characters humorously, without caricature.' No doubt because of his relationship with Emma, Hardy made the plot cheerful and at times lighthearted. Twenty years later he wrote to John Addington Symonds: 'The tragical conditions of life imperfectly denoted in *The Return of the Native* and some other stories of mine I am less and less able to keep out of my work. I often begin a story with the intention of making it brighter and gayer than usual; but the question of conscience soon comes in; and it does not seem right, even in novels, to wilfully belie one's own views.' In 1872 he finished a third novel, *A Pair of Blue Eyes*, setting it partly at Saint Juliot, and again relying on coincidences, some of which were gruesome and implausible. Since the book described a district which he was known to have visited, and since one of the characters was a young architect who had come to restore a church there, many people assumed that the tale was autobiographical. It certainly recalled Hardy's first visit to Saint Juliot: 'Thirteen to fifteen miles intervening between the railway terminus and the end of their journey had been gone over, when they began to pass along the brink of a valley some miles in extent, wherein the wintry skeletons of a more luxuriant vegetation than had hitherto surrounded them, proclaimed an increased richness of soil . . . ' In other and fewer words, the lands was less bleak. Hardy added a description of the lanes which he had explored with Emma: 'Then they rolled down a pass, the chocolate-coloured rocks forming on both sides . . . They mounted the last crest, and the way which was to be the end of their pilgrimage burst upon them. The ocean blueness deepened its colour as it stretched to the foot of the crags, where it terminated in a fringe of white – silent at this distance, though moving and heaving like the counterpane under a restless sleeper.'

In a preface to later editions, Hardy referred obliquely to his work at Saint Juliot: 'The following chapters were written at a time when the craze for indiscriminate church-restoration had just reached the remotest nooks of western England, where the wild and tragic features of the coast had long combined in perfect harmony with the crude Gothic art of the ecclesiastical buildings, scattered along it.' He referred also to tourism and his own custom of inventing place-names whereby Saint Juliot became Endlestow, and Boscastle became Castle Botrel. 'The shore and country about "Castle Botrel",' he wrote, 'is now getting well known . . . the spot, I may add, is among the furthest west of all those convenient corners wherein I have ventured to erect my theatre for these imperfect dramas of country life and passions.' He then cited the numinous aura of the district: 'The place is preeminently (for one person at least) the region of dream and mystery. The ghostly birds, the pall-like sea, the frothy wind, the eternal soliloquy of the waters, the bloom of a dark purple cast that seems to exhale from the shoreward precipices, in themselves lend to the scene an atmosphere like the twilight of a night vision.' In a second preface, written many years later, Hardy conceded that his Saint Juliot novel was immature, and that its readers were still trying to decode the fictitious place-names: 'To add a word on the topography of the romance in answer to questions . . . the mansion called 'Endlestow House' is to a large degree really existent, though it has to be looked for at a spot several miles south of the supposed site. The church, too, was made to be more open to the ocean than is the original.' (And the rectory became a vicarage).

In the year following publication of the novel, Hardy married Emma at Saint Peter's Church, Elgin Avenue, Paddington; the ceremony being conducted by the bride's uncle, Canon Gifford. After a honeymoon on the Continent, the couple lived at various lodgings in London, Dorset, and Somerset. Three years after that they made their first real home, at a riverside house in Sturminster Newton where, on fine summer evenings, they would drift downstream in a skiff, talking with scythesmen in the fields; but the drifters were ill-matched, and their idyll was brief. When they made a permanent home at Max Gate, the hideous Dorchester house which Hardy himself designed, the marriage was already doomed.

Much has been written about the relationship between Thomas and Emma Hardy. We know that he fell in love with several women, both before and after the marriage. His writings prove that, like the child in *Jude the Obscure*, he had been melancholy from earliest years. Parts of the novel come close to fulfilling Archibald MacLeish's prediction: 'To write constantly of death, of grief, of despair, of agony, of fear is almost to insure the failure of art . . . ' Even some of Hardy's admirers felt that he was spoiling a strong case by stating it too often. Although he denied it, Hardy was an atheist insofar as he rejected any deities of whom he had ever read or heard. The *agnostos theos* eluded him. 'I have,' he admitted, 'been looking for God for fifty years, and I think that if he had existed I should have discovered him.' Appalled by life's cruelty and injustice, he became

> A thinker of crooked thoughts upon life in the sere,
> And on that which consigns men to night after showing the
> day to them.

He seems not to have been unaware that belief and unbelief may follow a quasi-Calvinist or genetically predestined pattern, with external events tilting the scales. It is possible to share his bleak outlook while at the same time feeling that he expressed it too often and too monotonously. At the end of his life he resolved to do so no more. The last stanza of the last poem of his last book says:

> I'll let all be,
> And show to no man what I see.

Emma, by contrast, was religious and therefore hopeful: 'I have,' she affirmed, 'an ardent belief in Christianity and the life beyond this present one . . . '

A second source of discord was the class-consciousness in Victorian society. On first meeting her architect, Emma had noticed his 'slightly different accent'; a discreet reference to his background. Did Hardy contrive, either consciously or unconsciously, to tempt misfortune by marrying above his station? It is significant that several of his stories concerned a well-born woman and a man of humble birth. Two of the titles emphasise his preoccupation with social status: *A Group of Noble Dames* and *The Poor Man and the Lady*. Of Hardy's obsessive interest in men who are attracted by women of superior rank, Sir Arthur Quiller-Couch remarked: 'That he was born and bred liable to it – that the shadow of it dogged him – may, I think, be read in tale after tale of his . . . '

The disintegration of the marriage was witnessed by Dorothy Leech, a regular visitor to Max Gate: 'It appears to have been a happy marriage for several years,' she wrote, 'but as her husband's fame grew, his wife saw less and less of him. . . As she had come from a professional family, superior to that of Hardy, she liked people to refer to them as 'Mrs. Hardy and her husband' . . .' When Hardy entertained distinguished visitors, his wife 'had a habit of going up to the attic and remaining there until the guests had left'. She was so distracted by his embittered final novel, *Jude the Obscure*, that she went to London, hoping to stop the book's publication. Not without reason did the daughter of Hardy's doctor remark: 'Mrs. Emma Lavinia Hardy's mental condition progressively deteriorated . . . ' It is difficult to decide whether the deterioration was more a cause than an effect of domestic tension. In different circumstances the wife – even, perhaps, the husband – might have been reasonably happy. As it was, their mutual misery strengthened Hardy's belief that life is callous and purposeless: 'The President of the Immortals . . . had ended his sport with Tess.'

In order to secure some peace from the discord, Hardy built an external staircase whereby he could reach his study without entering the house. In 1912, shortly after her seventy-second birthday, Emma invaded the study. According to an old friend, Evelyn Evans, 'a scene of bitter recrimination took place. Next day she died of heart failure . . . Hardy was filled with remorse; at her Stinsford burial his flowers bore the words, 'From her lonely husband – with the old affection'. Bitterness ceased: the early Cornish rapture recovered its old magic, and his best-loved poetry was written in the years following Emma's death.' That is true; but it is likewise true that Hardy had already met Florence Emily Dugdale, who was thirty years younger than himself; and for five years the couple met and corresponded, taking care that Emma should not know of their relationship. In the year following Emma's death, Miss Dugdale went to live at Max Gate, acting as Hardy's housekeeper. Not long afterwards, having become his wife, Florence complained because he continually reread the diaries in which Emma had recorded his neglect of her. Haunted by remorse, Hardy revisited the places where he had courted Emma. It seems likely that he took with him the notebook in which Emma had described the happy moments of their early years together. From that rose-tinted pilgrimage came a sequence of love poems, a remarkable achievement by an old man, not least because it provided an exception to Robert Lynd's rule that Hardy's prosody resembled 'the clattering of milk churns'.

The Saint Juliot poems are indeed reflections from a nostalgic mirage, for Hardy never was so happy as he claimed to have been. Once again, Quiller-Couch told the truth: 'His widowhood had constructed a pure fairy-tale of that youthful time.' Hardy's diary serves as an introit to that fairy-tale: 'March 7 . . . arrived at St. Juliot Rectory . . . ' Then, decades later, looking back on that first journey to Lyonesse (his name for Cornwall), came the lyric which he rated as his finest:

> When I set out for Lyonesse
> A hundred miles away,
> The rime was on the spray,
> And starlight lit my lonesomeness
> When I set out for Lyonesse
> A hundred miles away.

Again: 'Received by a young lady in brown . . .' Then, decades later, his response to that reception:

> When I came back from Lyonesse
> With magic in my eyes,
> All marked with sure surmise,
> My radiance fair and fathomless
> When I came back from Lyonesse
> With magic in my eyes.

Now from Emma's memoir: 'I rode my pretty mare Fanny, and he walked by my side, and I showed him some more of the neighbourhood . . .' Then, decades later, from him:

> O the opal and the sapphire of that wandering western sea
> And the woman riding high above with bright hair flapping
>   fee . . .

Once more from Emma's memoir: 'We lost a tiny picnic-tumbler and there it is to this day no doubt between the two boulders.' Then, decades later, from the man who had dropped it:

I held the vessel to rinse in the fall,
Where it slipped and sank, and was past recall,
Though we stooped and plumbed the little abyss
With long bared arms. There the glass still is.

Now from Evelyn Evans: 'a scene of bitter recrimination took place. Next day she died of heart failure.' From the widower:

Why, then, latterly did we not speak,
Did we not think of those days long dead,
And ere your vanishing strive to seek
That time's renewal?

They did seek, but they never found; and now it was too late, because he had already completed his final visit to Fairyland:

I look back and see it there, shrinking and shrinking,
I look back at it amid the rain
For the very last time; for my sand is sinking
And I shall traverse love's old domain
Never again.

Never again in the flesh, yet often in spirit, for he tried to persuade himself that it had all been a dream:

Why go back to Saint Juliot? What's Juliot to me?

10
Sacred Mountains: Pembrokeshire

The track became so narrow that I decided I was following a sheep-path. This did not worry me, because the day was still young, and in any event I had deliberately chosen to wander on the summit of Prescelly Top, which the Welsh call *Foel Cwmcerwyn*, nearly eighteen hundred feet above Saint George's Channel. Not a cloud marred the sky. Not a building blocked the vista of turf and gorse and drystone walls. High overhead, a conclave of larks were glad to be alive, and said so, in their own lyrical language. Nothing else was audible until I moved, and then a breeze uttered its own tone of voice, scarcely loud enough to bend a grassblade.

Having lately arrived from North Devon, which is itself no

great way from North Cornwall, I noticed the resemblances between those two regions and parts of Pembrokeshire. One of the resemblances is linguistic and can be found on the Pembrokeshire lane from Saint David's to Trevine and also on the Cornish lane from Gerrans to Trewince, where the Welsh *tre* and the Cornish *trev* mean 'village or settlement'. Moreover, both of the lanes keep close to the sea; both are speckled with gorse; both pass stone houses and stone walls. No less remarkable is the resemblance between some of the people in the three counties, a legacy bequeathed by Celtic genes. During an earlier visit to the Prescelly Hills I had met a farmer who was evidently surprised when I asked whether he had a brother living in North Devon.

'I have not,' he replied.

'Or a cousin?'

'None of us lives in North Devon. Why do you ask?'

'Because for a moment I thought you were someone I knew.'

'Oh?'

'You're the same build, the same height, the same colouring, the same . . . ' There I paused lest he took me for a *Sais* who could not distinguish between an Arab and a Jew, or a Welshman and a Spaniard. If he had not already said that none of his family did live in North Devon, I would have greeted him as a brother of the man who kept a garage at Combe Martin, so closely the two resembled each other. Indeed, I would have ventured even further afield, asking whether any of his relatives lived in the Chilterns. On second thoughts I turned the question into a statement: 'If I may say so, you look very much like someone I knew forty years ago. His name was Gomm, and he kept the butcher's shop at Prestwood in Buckinghamshire. His family had lived there for centuries.' When the Welshman failed to understand why I had suddenly switched to Buckinghamshire, I explained that some of the Celts hid in the Chiltern beechwoods, trying to elude the Romans and Saxons, and that some of their descendants still resembled Matthew Arnold's 'dark Iberians'.

Those Celtic resemblances are enshrined in Pembrokeshire's soubriquet, 'Little England beyond Wales', a distillation of the history of a county whose capital was founded soon after the Norman Conquest. During the twelfth century a number of Flemish refugees settled at Rhos, in the neighbouring county of Carmarthenshire, where they married other immigrants – Norman, Saxon, Scandinavian – who ultimately became anglicised. The links with England were strengthened in 1138, when Pembrokeshire was created a palatinate or vice-regal area, and remained so until the reign of Henry VIII, who, in the words of Lord Herbert of Cherbury, 'reduc'd the lordship marchers to shire-ground'. However, the Marcher or frontier Lordship of Kemaes survives and is held *ex-officio* by the mayors of Newport, a small coastal town. Lord Cherbury quoted a petition from Welshmen who asked to be joined with England: 'We . . . inhabitants of that portion of the island which our invaders first called Wales, most humbly prostrate at your highness's feet, do crave to be receiv'd and adopted into the same laws and privileges which your other subjects enjoy . . . ' The King granted their request by signing three Statutes, the second being 'An Act for the laws and justice to be ministered in Wales in like form as it is in this realm'. Pembrokeshire acquired an unofficial border, the Landsker, stretching from Laugharne in Carmarthenshire to Newgale on the Pembrokeshire coast. North of that line the people spoke Welsh; south of it they spoke English. When I first visited Pembrokeshire, five hundred of its natives could not speak English; but they are all dead now, and many of the natives cannot speak Welsh.

Pembrokeshire's northern highlands are sometimes called mountains, but that is technically incorrect because (except in Scotland) no British hills are classified as mountains unless they reach a height of at least two thousand feet. Several maps mark the Pembrokeshire range as Mynydd Preseli (the Welsh *mynydd* may mean either 'hill' or 'mountain'), yet the same maps mark the summit of the range as Prescelly-Top. By whatever name, the rocks are chiefly of the Ordovician era, called after a Celtic tribe, the Ordovices. Although I never reached the highest point during maximum visibility, I do know that from it you can in clear weather see Dunkery Beacon (the summit of Exmoor, eighty miles to the south) and also Snowdon (the summit of Wales, eighty miles to the north).

It was on the Prescelly Hills, during the 1930s, that I met a party of gipsies; not the mechanised 'Tinkers' nor the quarter-breeds who work at fairs, but true gipsies, the Romanies, aloof, independent, not overfond of non-Romanies. Their caravans were as snug as the cabin of a horse-hauled barge, and their ponies cropped the turf nearby. Various garments had been spread to dry in the sun. Three of the small children were completely naked, and the women and girls went barefoot. The group looked very much like the one which Edmund Blunden met:

> The gipsies lolled and gossiped, and ate their stolen swedes,
> Made merry with mouth-organs, worked toys with piths of reeds;
> The old wives puffed their pipes, nigh as black as their hair,
> And not one of them all seemed to know the name of care.

Blunden's cameo is not a rose-tinted idyll, permissible when the sun shines, but misleading when the wind blows. Its veracity had been confirmed by W. H. Hudson's account of gipsies on Salisbury Plain during wild weather: 'In all this miserable year,' Hudson wrote, 'during which I have met and conversed with and visited many scores of gipsies, I have not found one who was not in a cheerful frame of mind, even when he was under a cloud with the police on his tracks, nor one with a cold, or complaining of an ache in his bones, or of indigestion.' In other words, a hale and active body provides its own central heating, whereof the thermostat is hindered, not helped, by double-glazing and electric blankets. Does one envy, or ought one to disapprove, people who ignore politics, elude schools, avoid towns, and generally give the impression of being happier and healthier than people for whom towns and schools and politics are of great importance?

The name 'gipsy' was originally *gipcyan*, meaning 'Egypt', the region from which the vagrants were supposed to have migrated. Anthropologists now believe that gipsies arrived from India by way of Iran, Turkey, and the Balkans. More than half of the gipsy vocabulary shows traces of dialects that are still spoken in northern India; for example, 'eye' is *akh* in Hindi, *yakh* in gipsy; 'black' is *kala* in Hindi, *kalo* in gipsy; 'butter' is *ghi* in Hindi, *ghil* in gipsy. Gipsies first reached Britain during the second half of the fifteenth century. King Henry VIII tried to curb their activities, and his daughter, Queen Elizabeth I, banished them on pain of death; yet they remained and are said to number thirty thousand, being most numerous in Surrey and Wales. Now I come to think of it, I have never visited the Prescelly Hills without making several detours, either purposely or by chance. A few roads do traverse part of the range, but a walker must rely on tracks and footpaths, many of which lead from nowhere in particular to anywhere in general. Few other parts of Wales excel the Prescelly Hills in their abundance of vistas, solitude, quietude, and glimpses of the sea. My favourite approach is from the east via Newcastle Emlyn and Cenarth, through Boncath to Clyn Ford and Mynnchlogddu; then along narrow lanes to Sittal (where John Wesley preached on the village green, the mayor of Pembroke having unlawfully forbidden him to preach at Saint Mary's Church), and so past The Kell, Haycastle Cross, Middle Mill, and finally to Saint David's, a city scarcely larger than a sizeable English village. What matter that the lanes are devious? They have never failed to please me. At Cenarth, for example, in a dell beside Afon Teifi, I found the oldest working watermill in Wales. At Charberton I met a veteran whose grandfather had witnessed the last invasion of Britain by a foreign power, when the French Revolutionaries landed an army of convicts near Carreg Wasted. At The Kell I saw a white blackbird. Near Haycastle Cross I tasted *cyflaith* or treacle toffee, made to an old Welsh recipe. At Saint David's I found sheep wandering through the Tourist Information Office. Elsewhere, especially on the lower slopes of the hills, I noticed many wood-larks, and on higher ground a cluster of fieldfares. At nine hundred feet I saw lizards sun-basking, and once or twice I encountered a posse of ponies, long-maned and reddish-brown, whose brood mares appeared to be running with a stallion. On the outskirts of Welsh Hook I talked with a farmer who was riding just such a pony.

'We collect and mark the foals in the autumn,' he told me. 'Very popular they are when they've been broken . . . that is, trained, you understand. And not only for children.' He patted his own pony. 'Eleven stone I weigh, yet she'll carry further than my legs could. I call her Rhiannon.'

'From the Mabinogion?'

'So you know?'

'I know that Rhiannon was a beautiful woman.'

'Do you know that she married the Prince of Dyfed?' The farmer smiled. 'I see you do not. However, it is something for an Englishman even to have heard of the Mabinogion. The Prince – or so the book says – went stag-hunting on the Prescelly Mountains, and after many adventures . . . I shouldn't wonder if some of them never happened . . . hey, you're the very man I want to see!'

I never heard the rest of the story, because the farmer rode off to meet the very man he wanted to see.

Some of the stones at Stonehenge came from the Prescelly Hills nearly three thousand years ago (the word *henge* is probably the Old English *hengen*, meaning in this instance 'to hang up' – a reference to the horizontal stones that rest on pillars). No one will ever know why Stonehenge was built, nor why Welsh stones were preferred to the ones which lay near the site in Wiltshire. Sir Cyril Fox believed that Stonehenge was a place of worship; part of it undoubtedly served as a cemetery. To primitive minds the Prescelly Hills may have seemed sacred and therefore a fitting source of building material for a shrine. The difficulty of moving massive blocks across miles of hilly country persuaded some geologists that the movement had been made not by machineless men but by Pleistocene ice-sheets which left the blocks stranded in Wiltshire. A later study of ice movements proved that this could not have occurred. Finally, in 1923, Dr. H. H. Thomas discovered that the three chief varieties of Stonehenge bluestones exactly match those in the Prescelly Hills, and that the only place at which all three varieties stand close to one another is an area of about one square mile on the eastern edge of the range, between Foel

Trigarn and Carn Meinhi. How, then, did the stones reach Salisbury Plain, and by what route? Various answers have been given, and various experiments have been made, using rafts, canoes, and schoolboys from Bryanston and Canford. The details of those journeys are technical. To me, a layman, the most plausible theory runs as follows: having been hewn with bone tools, the blocks were hauled on sledges to Milford Haven, whence they were shipped across the Severn Sea, either on rafts or in canoes. They reached their present site by following the rivers Avon and Frome and Wylye, with only a relatively few miles of sledging over the last lap. We rightly marvel at the masons who built the west front of Wells Cathedral and the vaulting roof of King's College Chapel; how much more do we marvel at the men who sawed the rock with bone, dragged the cargo overland on sledges, and then ferried it across miles of turbulent water. If only by tracing the stones to Pembrokeshire, archaeologists have outdated Dr. Johnson's assertion: 'All that is known of the ancient state of Britain is contained in a few pages. We can know no more than what the old writers have told us.'

During World War I the Royal Air Force demanded that Stonehenge be demolished because it stood in the way of aircraft. Fortunately, the site was bought by Sir Cecil Chubb, who in 1918 gave it to the nation. When I last saw the monument it appeared to be unapproachable, heavily defended against vandals. When I first saw it, in 1937, it stood alone on a knoll, sans hedge or wall or railings, so that anyone could set his hand upon the stones and thereby feel – like Siegfried Sassoon – the touch of

> Time, that anticipates eternities,
> And has an art to resurrect the rose.

11
A Shepherd's Life: Hampshire

The signposts were useless. None of them named my destination. The man whom I eventually consulted was likewise useless, for he told me to reach a certain crossroads and to enquire there. On reaching the roads, I found no one of whom to enquire. In short, the last part of the mission was becoming as difficult as the first, which had begun several weeks earlier, when I tried to discover where my destination lay. Meanwhile, I waited at the crossroads, wondering how much further I must travel before I reached the home of a shepherd whom W. H. Hudson had made famous.

Hudson was one of those active contemplatives whom Walt Whitman classified as 'Shepherds, out-of-door natural persons, men living close to the elements'. Hudson himself expressed it more brusquely, saying that he had been 'born and bred in a semi-barbarous district among horsemen of the pampas'. In 1869, at the age of twenty-eight, he left Argentina and settled in England, where he set up as a naturalist who studied humanity as closely as he studied flora and fauna. Books about country life, however, seldom earn their authors' bread and butter, so he spent many years living at various apartments and boarding houses which his wife kept in London. Throughout those years he explored a large part of southern England, from Sussex to Cornwall. Mostly he went on foot; always he sought cheap lodgings, at any rate until he was fifty years old, when a Civil List pension of £3 a week relieved him of the need to rely solely on small and uncertain royalties from books. His best-loved work, *A Shepherd's Life*, sprang from a chance meeting while he was staying at the Silchester house of a woman whose father had been a shepherd. 'I fell in with the old shepherd,' Hudson explained, 'whose anecdotes and reflections proved so interesting that I fell into the habit of putting them down in my notebook . . . ' The note-taking was assiduous yet leisurely: 'It came to me in conversations at intervals during several years, with the shepherd . . . I would sit and smoke with him, and if he were in a talking mood I would tell him where I had been . . . on the heath, in the woods, anywhere, on the chance of its reminding him of something worth hearing of his past life.' The first fruits of that note-taking were two articles for *Longman's Magazine*; the final harvest was *A Shepherd's Life*, an evocation of Victorian rural England, with special reference to the shepherd Caleb Bawcombe, who lived long enough to receive a copy of the work, inscribed by the author. Without ever becoming a sociological tract, Hudson's book depicts the work and environment of the shepherd and some of his relatives and friends. With a naturalist's eye and an artist's imagination, Hudson discusses the sheep, the dogs, the plants, the wild creatures, the look of the land by day and at night, in summer and in winter, fine weather and foul. Ernest Rhys rated *A Shepherd's Life* as 'the best prose pastoral we have in English'.

After rereading the book, I decided to visit the district in which the shepherd had spent most of his life. It seemed easy enough to find the village and to ask about the shepherd, because Hudson stated that the latter was called Caleb Bawcombe, and that the former was called Winterbourne Bishop: 'The nearest town,' he added, 'or easiest to get to, being Salisbury twelve miles away.' I was therefore perplexed when neither the Wiltshire gazetteers nor the standard work on English place names mentioned Winterbourne Bishop. On consulting a friend who lived in Wiltshire, I learned that Winterbourne Bishop was a fictitious name; the true name being Martin. Since the place lay only a dozen miles from the capital of Wiltshire, I once again turned to the Wiltshire gazetteers, and once again failed to find what I sought. Wiltshire contained no Martin. Fortunately, the place name book proved more helpful, stating that Martin was the Old English '*mere-tun*' or 'settlement by a lake', but it was not in Wiltshire; it was in Hampshire. So far as I could discover, Martin used to lie near the eastern border of the kingdom of Wessex, which changed shape with the fortunes of war. In 1895 a new border was drawn, transferring to Hampshire the three Wiltshire parishes of Whitbury, South Damerton, and Martin, thereby creating the so-called 'Martin peninsula' which projects part of Hampshire to within a few miles of the capital of Wiltshire. Although this revision was made before *A Shepherd's Life* appeared, Hudson gave the book a subtitle, *Impressions of the South Wiltshire Downs*. He may have justified himself on two grounds: first, that Martin had been in Wiltshire throughout most of the shepherd's life; second, that fictitious names helped to preserve the privacy of the place and of the person (in his magazine articles he called the village Lupton).

Having solved the mystery, I did at last find the village, wondering en route whether my first impressions of it would tally with Hudson's: 'I cannot think,' he wrote, 'that any person for whom it has no associations, no secret interest, would, after looking at this village . . . care to make his home there . . . for it has no special attractions, and is away from any road . . . at a distance from anywhere.' A second visit confirmed his poor opinion. Clearly, therefore, it was the shepherd, not the village, that attracted Hudson: 'Had it not been for this feeling he produced in me I should not, I imagine, have cared to stay long . . . ' Later visits, however, made the heart grow fonder: 'As it was, I did stay, then came again, and found it was growing on me . . . ' Martin, in short, acted like a magnet: 'From the time I left the turnpike road to go to the last two and a half to three miles by the side road I would gaze eagerly for the sight of my destination long before it could possibly be seen; until, on gaining the summit of a low, intervening down, the wished scene would be disclosed – the vale-like, wide depression, with its line of trees, blue-green in the distance, the flecks of red and grey colour of the houses among them – and at that sight there would be a sense of elation, like that of coming home.' Some people find the Wiltshire Downs bleak and monotonous; not so William Cobbett, who chose the district as one of his two favourite landscapes: 'My choice has always been very much divided between the woods of Sussex and the downs of Wiltshire.'

On first sighting Martin I wondered what changes had occurred since Hudson described it: 'Real houses are none . . . unless the small farmhouses are considered better than cottages, and the rather mean-looking rectory . . . in the middle part, where the church stands in its green churchyards, a few of the cottages are close together, almost touching, then farther apart, twenty yards or so, then farther still, forty or fifty yards. They are small, old cottages: a few have seventeenth century dates cut in stone tablets on their fronts . . . ' On entering Martin I decided that the modern houses did not wholly outdate Hudson's description. Martin, in fact, is set beside a long street, many of the buildings being more than a century old; some, several centuries old. The village shop is also a Post Office. On a knoll set back from the street, the church is well tended. At the eastern end of the village a lane leads leftward past a few ancient cottages and farms. The rest is fields and downland, creating the impression that Martin stands, as Hudson said, 'at a distance from anywhere'.

Seeking advice from the vicar, I was told that he had lately retired, but would be found nearby, decorating his new home. In reply to my questions he told me to consult Mrs. Eleanor Whitelegge, a widow, who had lived at Martin for more than forty years and was very knowledgeable about its history. 'Before you go,' the vicar said, 'you must visit our church.' He paused, but did not mention vandals. 'The key is at the Post Office. Say you've been to see me.'

In the churchyard I found the grave of William Lawes, whose headstone stated that he was the original of Caleb Bawcombe's father, Isaac, and that he died in 1866, aged eighty-six. Hudson described Isaac Bawcombe as 'a very fine specimen of a man, both physically and morally'. At a time when many elderly farmhands were paupers, a charitable bequest enabled Isaac to acquire a cottage, a suit of clothes, and sufficient food and fuel. Moreover, his former master still employed him at light duties. In Hudson's words: 'Isaac found himself very well off indeed, and he enjoyed his prosperous state for twenty-six years.' The old man's death was predictable, occurring shortly after his wife's: 'He, too, began to droop; and soon, before the year was out, he followed her, because, as the neighbours said, they had always been a loving pair and could not 'bide' without the other.' Inside the church, on the left of the altar, I noticed a shepherd's crook which, so the villagers like to believe, had belonged either to Isaac or to Caleb.

From the church I walked a quarter-mile to visit Mrs. Whitelegge, a delightful lady, who shared my own interest in Hudson and the shepherd. While collecting his material, she told me, Hudson lodged at Harris's Farm near the church; the house still stands, but the upper storey has been altered. Mrs. Whitelegge then mentioned a local woman who possessed some notes on the subject, made long ago by an antiquary. The woman so valued these notes that she was unwilling to part with them, but she did agree to bring them to Mrs. Whitelegge, who copied the relevant sections for me. These proved that Isaac Bawcombe really was William Lawes, and that his son, Caleb, really was James Lawes. The notes also confirmed other facts in Hudson's narrative, notably a lawsuit which Caleb brought against a fellow-villager, Malachi Martin, whom Hudson called Elijah Raven, adding that he was mean, sordid, greedy, tyrannous', and that he occupied a house 'situated about the centre of the village street . . . a quaint, old, timbered house, little bigger than a cottage . . . '. Elijah shared this house with an old man who did the cooking and sewing. When the man died, Elijah continued to live there alone, probably in some disorder because 'not only was he a bachelor, but he would never allow any woman inside his house'. Elijah, at all events, bullied the other villagers, who were therefore astonished when he volunteered to act as honorary secretary of a benefit society which they had founded as an insurance against illness and age and death. Believing that the sinner had at last repented of his wickedness, the subscribers accepted Elijah's offer, but were soon disillusioned when he withheld a sick benefit to which Caleb was entitled. No other course being open to them, the villagers collected five pounds – a large sum for such people in those years – thereby enabling Caleb to consult a Salisbury solicitor. According to Hudson's narrative, the shepherd won the case: 'Bawcombe got his six weeks' sick pay and expenses and about three pounds beside . . . ' According to Mrs. Whitelegge's notes, a Salisbury solicitor's ledger recorded payment of six shillings and eightpence, by James Lawes alias Caleb Bawcombe, for taking an affidavit in a case similar to the one which Hudson recounted.

Unlike George Borrow, whose books blend fact with fiction, Hudson reported only what he believed to be true. He revealed for example, that Caleb had spent twelve months as a shepherd in Dorset, until homesickness proved too strong: 'His mind was set on going back to his own native village and to his own people.' The decision required courage because employment in Dorset was assured, whereas at Martin it might be unobtainable. Nevertheless, back to Martin he went: 'And so when the long year was ended he took his crook and set out over the hills and valleys, followed by a cart containing his "sticks" and wife and children. And at home with his old parents and his people he was happy once more; in a short time he found a place as head-shepherd, with a cottage in the village, and followed his flock to the old familiar down, and everything again was as it had been at the beginning of life, and as he desired it to be even to the end.'

Although I failed to find anyone who had met Caleb Bawcombe, Mrs. Whitelegge did introduce me to a villager, Mrs. Ida Cox, who had met Hudson while he was writing *A Shepherd's Life*. I can repreat Mrs. Cox's words almost verbatim: 'Mr. Hudson wore a Norfolk jacket which impressed us children because our schoolmaster wore one too. We called Mr. Hudson "the bird man" and sometimes "the flower man" because he was always asking about those things. One day he heard of some white scented orchids in the district, but when he asked a gamekeeper where to find them the man shook his head and said, "If I do tell you, you'll pick 'em and that'll be the end of 'em".' Mrs. Cox's impressions of Hudson – as tall, friendly, distinguished – tallied with Ernest Rhys's memory of 'an eagle face, keen scrutinising look, alert head . . . he was as simple a guest to entertain as one could wish'. Mrs. Cox told me that the Martin people envied Hudson because his landlady at Harris's Farm was regarded as the best cook in the village; she had, in fact, served as cook at a large house in Buckinghamshire.

'What,' I asked Mrs. Cox, 'were his lodgings like?'

'All I can remember is, taking a peep at the sitting-room. It had two fireplaces, one at each end.'

'That sounds as though the room had originally been two,' I said.

All told, Hudson spent about ten weeks at Martin, exploring the countryside, questioning the people, and writing parts of the book. He also lodged awhile at another Wiltshire village, Bindon. Since Victorian cottagers were not as a rule avid readers, I felt no surprise when Mrs. Cox admitted that the publication of *A Shepherd's Life* caused little stir in the village. The wider world, by contrast, showed more interest. 'All sorts of visitors arrived,' Mrs. Cox said. 'We had professors and newspaper reporters and people in cars that were often breaking down.' So far from subsiding, the interest in *A Shepherd's Life* grew stronger and wider. During the 1980s the *Daily*

Telegraph remarked that the book 'is still popular among an urban generation hungry for news of green pastures, quiet lanes, thatched cottages, old skills'. Hudson certainly described those things; but he never indulged a rose-tinted reverie about the good old days. Time after time he cited the plight of the rural proletariat: 'Unemployed men of the village . . . would be put to flint-gathering in the fields, their wages being four shillings a week.' Such a wage at such a time would barely keep a man from starvation. Glancing further back, to Caleb's youth, Hudson cited the hungry labourers who were either hanged or transported for stealing a sheep. Hudson's compassion did not prevent him from arraigning the 'sedition-mongers, the Socialists, the furious denouncers of all landlords'. Caleb himself became a victim of his own activity: 'Early in life he "caught a chill" through long exposure to wet and cold in winter; this brought on rheumatic fever and a malady of the thigh, which finally affected the whole of the limb and made him lame for life.' Despite the affliction, he followed the calling. At lambing time, often in bitter weather, he spent whole days and nights alone with the sheep, living in a wheeled hut on the Downs, where he cooked his meals and succoured any ailing ewes or lambs. Like most countryfolk at that time, he retained a firm faith in life, looking beyond the ups-and-downs of Wiltshire. He had, said Hudson, 'fawnlike eyes that gazed steadily at you as one may gaze through the window, open back and front, of a house at the landscape beyond . . . ' This far-sightedness coexisted with a closer vision: 'He had a curiously tender feeling about the little wild birds.'

Hudson, then, saw Victorian life as it really was, at the manor house, at the farmhouse, at the shepherd's cottage. He saw it as an artist sees it, not as a politician. He described rather than dissected, finding nothing in the established order that could not be amended by the order itself. His book, therefore, survives as a work of art, not as a piece of propaganda, for although statistics can litanise wages and diet and hours of work, they cannot, as Hudson could, depict the decline and fall of a Wiltshire manor house: 'First a monks' house, it fell at the Reformation to some greedy gentleman who made it his dwelling, and doubtless in later times it was used as a farm-house. Now a house most desolate, dirty, and neglected, with cracks in the walls which threaten ruin, standing in a wilderness of weeds, tenanted by a poor working man whose wages are twelve shillings a week, and his wife and eight small children. The rent is eighteen-pence a week – probably the lowest-rented manor-house in England, though it is not very rare to find such places tenanted by labourers.' Similarly, no statistics can convey the kind of information which Hudson supplied: 'One day in September, while sauntering over Mare Down, I passed three flocks of sheep, all with many bells, and I noticed that each flock produced a distinctly different sound or effect, owing doubtless to a different number of big and little bells in each; and it struck me that any shepherd on a dark night, or if taken blindfold over the downs, would be able to identify his own flocks by the sound.'

The sheep-walks near Martin are almost as lonely as when Caleb pastured his flocks there. At the southern end of the village a lane to Cranborne soon reaches open downland, not greatly changed since Hudson wrote of a 'wide, empty land, with nothing on it but a furze-bush; or where I had gained the summit of the down, and to get a little higher still stood on the top of one of its many barrows, a sight of a distant village, its low, grey or reddish-brown cottages half hidden among its few trees . . . That emptiness seemed good for the mind and body; and I could spend long hours idly sauntering or sitting and lying on the turf . . . thinking of nothing, or only of one thing – that it was a relief to have no thought about anything.' At such moments Hudson shared the experience of Richard Rolle, the mediaeval mystic, who discovered that, when he seemed to be asleep, his heart was wide awake: *Ego dormio et cor meum vigilat*. On the Downs above Martin a walker understands why Hudson felt that to return thither was like 'coming back to nature and solitude and the freedom of a wide earth and sky'. Progress has not yet imposed the modernity which Hudson dreaded: 'If some ostentatious person had come to this strangely quiet spot and raised a staring, big house, the sight of it in the landscape would have made it impossible to have such a feeling as I have described.' He admired the old Wiltshire cottages: 'There are, I imagine, few places in England where the humble homes of the people have so great a charm. Undoubtedly, they are darker inside and not so convenient to live in as the modern box-shaped, red-brick, slate-roofed cottages which have spread a wave of ugliness over the country; but they do not offend – they please the eye . . . They are weathered and coloured by sun and wind and rain. They appear related to the trees amid which they stand, to the rivers and meadows, to the sloping downs at the side, and to the sky and clouds over all.'

During his Wiltshire explorations Hudson spent some happy hours in Gread Ridge Wood, a remote haven, frequented only by gamekeepers: 'It was a joy to me,' he said, 'to find such a spot in England, so wild and solitary.' That wild solitude led Caleb Bawcombe to speak the words with which Hudson concluded *A Shepherd's Life*: 'I don't say I want to have my life again, because 'twould be sinful. We must take what is sent. But if 'twas offered me and I was told to choose my work, I'd say, Give me my Wiltsheer Downs and let me be a shepherd there all my life long.'

12
Good Taste: Rutland

If, in Surrey, you say; 'I'm just off to see Mary Brown'; and if, in Staffordshire, you say: 'I'm just off to see Joan Smith', people will assume that you are about to meet someone; but if, in Rutland, you say: 'I'm just off to see Edith Weston', people will not assume that you are about to meet someone. Rutland, in short, is in many ways peculiar, not least because it no longer exists.

Formerly called *Roteland* or 'the land of Rota's tribe', Rutland was at one time an administrative district rather than a county, which is why Domesday Book assessed it as lying partly in Northamptonshire and partly in Lincolnshire. During the reign of King John, Rutland did become a county, the smallest in England. Later still, it became one of the Shires which the *Oxford Dictionary* defines as 'the name of a hunting country . . . ' Combining scholarship with venery, the dictionary qualifies its definition: 'Several packs which hunt within those limits, however, belong to the "Shires", whereas a district of the Belvoir is in Lincolnshire, and to ride with the Belvoir is certainly to be hunting in the "Shires".' When Hugo Meynell became Master of the Quorn in 1753, the Shires acquired such a reputation as a fox-hunting district that hunting folk called them the Shires, but the rest of Britain they called the Provinces. Meynell himself is remembered in the song of the Quorn Hunt:

> That sire of the Chase – our crack Nimrod, old Meynell –
> Once said to a famed brother sportsman at Quorn,
> That 'the fame and the fun of a Leicestershire kennel
> Should cease when the sun ceased to gladden the morn.'

Belvoir Castle, seat of the Dukes of Rutland, stands on a hill just across the Leicestershire border. After three rebuildings in two centuries, the castle is best described as mock-baronial. The Duke of Rutland's eldest son bears a courtesy title, Marquis of Granby, whence the numerous public houses of that name, especially in the Vale of Belvoir. During the 1980s the Coal Board and the Miners' Union were still hoping to transform this beautiful Vale into a vast colliery, with new roads, heavy traffic, and an influx of highly-paid workers whose ways and means clash with those of farm workers. During the 1960s Leicestershire tried to destroy Rutland by swallowing it. With Sir Kenneth Ruddle at their head, the men of Rutland defied and eventually defeated their greedy neighbour. In 1973, a Philistine Government did destroy Rutland by merging it with Leicestershire. As a consolation, the county retains its ancient name in the Rutland County Museum; in the Leicestershire and Rutland Society for the Blind; in the Leicestershire, Northamptonshire and Rutland branch of the National Farmers' Union; and in a reservoir, Rutland Water.

Defoe's *Tour Through the Whole Island of Great Britain* dismissed Rutland with twenty words: 'We enter'd Rutlandshire, remarkable for being the least county in England, having but two market towns, viz. Okeham and Uppingham.' As a brief afterthought, Defoe admitted that Rutland was 'famous for the abundance of fine seats of the gentlemen'. Some of those seats were built of stone from Barnack Quarry in Northamptonshire; others, of the pink-and-brown Ketton Stone which went to build the Law Courts in London and to repair the cathedrals in Exeter and York. Many of the Rutland cottages are of a warm brown ironstone. The stone from a Rutland quarry at Clipsham is so durable that it was used to re-face several colleges at Oxford and Cambridge. Two centuries ago a considerable number of the cottagers were smallholders, as described by John Crutchley's survey of Rutland: 'There are a great many cottagers, by which I mean, occupiers of small portions of land just sufficient to enable them to keep one or two cows, without preventing them from working constantly as day labourers . . . the benefit of it is felt by the cottagers themselves to the greatest degree . . . ' One of Defoe's contemporaries composed a Rutland panegyric which sounds like an estate agent's brochure:

> The under-lying vale shews with delight
> A thousand beauties, at one sight,
> No pencil's art can such a landskip feign,
> And Nature's self scarce yields the like again.
> Few situations may with this compare,
> A fertile soil and a salubrious air.

The older guidebooks implied that Rutland's sole claim to fame was its smallness. One nineteenth-century survey of agriculture began with the words: 'This least of English counties . . . ' Another survey stated that Rutland contained 'only fifty-three parishes and four hamlets'. Rutland was undoubtedly small. You could walk across its widest part in just over four hours, and across its longest part in about the same time. The population of 23,000 was roughly the same as the present population of Aylesbury in Buckinghamshire and of Bridgwater in Somerset, two relatively small towns. Rutland remained underrated until the 1950s, when W. G. Hoskins announced: 'Rutland is a small part of England as she used to be before the Industrial Revolution – unsoiled, clean, full of fine buildings, of country smell, of neatness, order and natural good taste.' Dr. Hoskins's eulogy is still valid. There are no industrial zones in this ancient county, no suburbs, no large towns. Rutland's work is agriculture, without which there would be no work at all, because there would be no workers, because there would be no food wherewith to feed them. Not even technology can convert bulldozers into bread.

Whenever I visit Rutland I make for Uppingham, following a route so zany that I advise you not to seek it on the map. First I reach Stoke Dry, the birthplace of a leading Gunpowder Plotter, Sir Everard Digby, whom King James I knighted at Belvoir Castle. Turning from Anglicanism to Romanism, Digby spent large sums of money on hatching the plot. When it failed he was arrested and condemned to death. While awaiting trial he wrote several casuistical letters, saying that he saw nothing wrong in trying to assassinate most members of the Royal Family and of both Houses of Parliament: 'If,' he declared, 'I had thought there had been the least sin in the Plot, I would not have been in it for all the world . . . '

My next destination, Edith Weston, was named after Earl Godwin's daughter, Queen Eadyth, on whom Edward the Confessor bestowed a large area of Rutland. Robert of Gloucester described the Queen as 'the gracious rose of Godwin's thorny stem'. The lady must have been erudite as well as gracious, because a contemporary historian said that he had often met her during his schooldays at Westminster, where she tested his knowledge of Latin grammar. The countryside near Edith Weston has been adroitly landscaped by the Anglian Water Authority at Rutland Water, England's largest artificial lake. As though to refute a widespread belief that the Shires are uniformly flat, the high ground near Rutland Water overlooks the Welland Valley, and large tracts of Leicestershire and Northamptonshire. The signposts likewise refute the fallacy: Burley-on-the-Hill, Burrough-on-the-Hill, Easton-on-the-Hill, Illston-on-the Hill, Witham-on-the-Hill, Waltham-on-the-Wolds. The numerous place-names containing *thorp* and *by* are relics of colonies that were established by

Nordic pirates who landed on the east coast, whence they rowed their ships up-river into the heart of the Shires.

Some villages seem to become utterly depopulated whenever I visit them. Such a one is Llanfair Clydogau in Carmarthenshire; another is Shipley in Sussex; another, Caldbeck in Cumberland; another, Idlecote in Warwickshire; a fifth, Welcombe in Devon. The sixth such village is Edith Weston. I have entered it several times at an hour when I might have expected to see a housewife on her way to market, or a child playing in a garden, or a face at a window; but always I arrived and departed without seeing a soul.

From Edith Weston the car-free lanes lead to Lyddington, whose village green and single street are lined with ironstone cottages, some of them bearing the date of their birth. The only blemish is a brace of bungalows. Lyddington achieved some importance when the mediaeval Bishops of Lincoln acquired a manor house there (rebuilt *c.* 1480 by Bishop Russell, who also rebuilt the church nave). In 1547 the manor house passed to Henry VIII and ultimately to the Elizabethan Cecils, one of whom converted it into a hospice or bede house for ten poor men. To-day it is an Ancient Monument, admirably restored.

I like to walk from Lyddington to Uppingham, through England at its most beneficent. Uppingham is a small market town with a miniature market place. The parish church stands as it were with one foot in the town and with the other in the fields. Most of the houses are handsome, and the best-looking is the Tudor House in High Street. Boys from the public school conduct themselves with amiable decorum, as also do the people who either live at Uppingham or go shopping there. The credit for this happy state of affairs belongs partly to the school itself, which owns considerable property in the town. Uppingham School was founded in 1584 by Archdeacon Johnson, who endowed exhibitions to Oxford and Cambridge. The curriculum evidently suited his own son, for it taught him Greek, Latin, Hebrew, Spanish, Italian, rhetoric, geometry, and music; all of which the child mastered so swiftly that at the age of thirteen he went up to Emmanuel College, Cambridge. Archdeacon Johnson intended his foundation to be a small grammar school for the sons of local farmers and gentry; and so it remained until Edward Thring made it famous. When Thring became headmaster in 1853 the school still occupied the original Tudor building near the church; the number of pupils was twenty-three; and it is said that one of the three masters spent most of his time mending quill pens. Despite opposition from some of the school governors, Thring began to enlarge the school, not for enlargement's sake, but in the spirit of Dr. Arnold, who said of Rugby: 'It is *not* necessary that this should be a school of three hundred, or one hundred, or fifty boys; but it is necessary that it should be a school of Christian gentlemen.' Thring obtained and soon over-spent a large sum of money on the new buildings. Remembering his own schooldays in Eton's crowded Long Chamber, he allotted a study to each boy, thereby following the advice of Queen Elizabeth's tutor, Roger Ascham, whose treatise, *The Schoolmaster*, said: 'The child must take a paper book, and sitting in some place, where no man shall prompt him, by himself, let him translate into English his former lessons.' Thring limited the size of each class to twenty-five boys, and the total number at the school to three hundred. Being an enlightened pedagogue, he kept the cane as a deterrent. When several boys arrived late at the start of the Easter term, pleading that they had misread the railway timetable, Thring caned them *pour encourager les autres*; and it was proof of Uppingham's new importance that *Punch* mentioned the incident: 'Mr. Thring,' it said, 'seemed to know how to manage boys, and if he did not train their minds, he made them mindful of their trains.' Among the eminent alumni were Cecil Sharp, the collector of English folk songs, and E.W. Hornung, the creator of Raffles. The main buildings of Uppingham School resemble a college at Oxford or Cambridge. Although not quite a Merton Street, the approach to the school is quiet, well-planned, and flanked by handsome stone houses. The entrance has a three-storey rectangular tower above an arched gateway leading to quadrangles and lawns. The museum and the chapel are good Victorian Gothic; the science block, good Victorian Jacobean. Other of the school buildings occupy other parts of the town.

From the centre of Uppingham you can within a few minutes reach some of the finest hunting country in Britain, planted with coverts by nineteenth-century landowners who wished many foxes to breed therein. Fox-hunting in Rutland is as popular as ever it was; in fact, it is more popular because more widely shared. All sorts and conditions of men and women attend the Meet, and many of them follow hounds, either mounted or on foot. You will see the postman's daughter and the squire's lady alongside prosperous yeomen and not-so-prosperous colonels. Between autumn and spring the county echoes John Gay's *Reveille*:

> The morning wakes, the huntsman sounds,
> At once rush forth the joyful hounds.
> They seek the wood with eager pace,
> Through bush, through brier, explore the chase.

According to the Masters of Fox Hounds Association, the only packs which may properly call themselves Shire packs are the Belvoir, the Cottesmore, the Quorn, and the Fernie. Since my own hunting days ended long ago, and were confined to the South Oxfordshire and the Old Berkley, I shall merely repeat some gossip which I heard at Uppingham, as follows: The Quorn has the finest hunting country, the Pytchley has the largest territory, the Belvoir has the best hounds.

I retain two pleasant memories of England's smallest county, wherein the lanes seem to be perennially off the beaten track. The first memory is of a summer morning when I followed the lane from Thorpe-by-the-Water to its thirstily-named neighbour, Dry Stoke. Having lately left the Great North Road, I halted to enjoy the stillness; seeing no one except a farmer and his dog, less than a hundred yards from where I sat. The farmer, who had not noticed me, pushed back his cap, lit his pipe, and for several minutes leaned on a gate, thinking (as I hoped) such pleasant thoughts as such pleasant surroundings might arouse in pleasant people. Then he turned to his dog, saying: 'What do *you* think about it, eh?' The question, though cryptic, sounded cheerful; and away he went, a good shepherd among his sheep.

My second memory is of a winter evening when the light was fading as I entered Uppingham, where firelit curtains carved warm patterns on rinsed pavements. Only one car was visible, parked in the little square. No townsfolk at all were visible until a door opened, a woman exclaimed, 'What a night!', and a child hurried down the street. From the square I heard the sound of distant sheep and nothing else except the rain pattering and the gutters gushing. At the hotel a receptionist assured me that dinner and a bed were available. Two hours later, after an excellent dinner in restful surroundings – only five other people were staying the night – I took coffee alongside the widow of an Uppingham master ('Happy memories,' she sighed, 'are very sad, but I would not be without them') and also an elderly man who in his youth had hunted with the local pack and was looking forward to the chase next day ('I can't really afford it,' he admitted, 'but by giving up wine and by smoking only two pipes a day I just manage to come here once a year').

Soon after ten o'clock I opened my bedroom window and peered on to the square. The sheep were silent now, but the rain was still audible, lulling me to sleep.

13
An Incomparable Young Man: Oxfordshire

Several villages may claim to be the most beautiful in Oxfordshire. One thinks of Ewelme, Clifton Hampden, Minster Lovell. My own short list would include Great Tew, which lies in a secluded corner of the county, only a few miles from the Warwickshire border. There is not a single ugly building in the village. Most of the cottages are thatched, and all are ancient. The inn, The Falkland Arms, was named after Lucius Cary, second Viscount Falkland, whose character and achievements raised Great Tew from obscurity to fame.

Lucius Cary was born in or about the year 1610, at The Priory in Burford, the home of his maternal grandfather, Sir Lawrence Tanfield, Lord Chief Baron. Lucius's father was

Lord Deputy of Ireland, which explains why the son studied a while at Trinity College, Dublin. According to Edward Hyde, Lucius then went up to St. John's College, Cambridge; according to Wood's *Athenae Oxonienses*, he scored an academic hat-trick by proceeding to Exeter College, Oxford. Before coming of age he inherited The Priory from Tanfield, whose fifteen-year-old daughter had married the first Viscount Falkland, whereafter the bridegroom squandered most of his wife's money as well as most of his own, which so angered Tanfield that, instead of bequeathing The Priory to his daughter, he diverted it to her son, who soon afterwards angered his own father by marrying Lettie Morison, a girl of ancient family but with no dowry, sister of his friend Henry Morison (the two men were eulogised in Jonson's ode 'To the Immortal Memory and Friendship of that noble pair, Sir Lucius Cary and Sir H. Morison'). Following this estrangement, Lucius went to Holland, and would have become a professional soldier there, had not his father soon afterwards died, leaving a quantity of debts which forced the son to sell The Priory to Mr. Speaker Lenthall. Returning to Great Tew, the new Viscount began at once to fulfil his responsibilities as a landowner and to increase his reputation as a scholar. The ordeals which lay ahead, both for himself and for his country, could not then be foreseen nor even imagined.

Falkland's village still wears what may be called an old-world look. Shaded by trees and flanked by a green, the cottages are built of local stone, and none is an exact replica of the rest. Their roofs are either steeply thatched or covered with thin slates of yellowish stone. The walls vary in colour from grey-brown to rich ochre. The gardens have trim hedges; the diamond-paned windows have mullions with drip-stones; the doors have spandrels and stone cornices. Approaching Great Tew from Warwickshire, you follow a tree-lined lane which curves gracefully as it enters the village. On the left stands an eighteenth-century house; on the right, a grass path leads to the church, embowered among many kinds of trees that were planted by John Loudon, a nineteenth-century landscape gardener, who for several years lived at Tew Park Farm. Loudon was only twenty-five years old when the lord of the manor, General Stratton, commissioned him so to recreate Great Tew that the mediaeval church and the new manor house should blend more nearly with the parklands and cottages and farms. Loudon was given 132 labourers wherewith to execute his plans for roads, drains, farms, and trees; in short, he was free to practise what he called 'landscape husbandry', a blend of aesthetics and economics, at a time when landowners could afford to make their estates beautiful as well as profitable. Loudon himself wrote a treatise on forestry, emphasising the importance of site and pattern: 'The natural form and outline of a tree can only be ascertained when the tree stands alone.' After passing from General Stratton to Matthew Boulton, the village received further improvements; this time by an architect, Thomas Rickman, who adorned each cottage with a pleasing porch. A vicarage and a new school were built; the ancient stocks were preserved; and one of the cottages became a Post Office-cum-shop.

Returning from the church to the lane, you pass a few old houses and then a green knoll overlooking a row of seventeenth-century cottages. Bearing left, you reach a winding cul-de-sac, flanked by more cottages, some of which, when I saw them fifty years ago, were decaying because the lord of the manor had been taxed out of his ability to repair them. During the 1970s, however, the village was declared an Outstanding Conservation Area, eligible for a grant from the Historic Buildings Council. The lord of the manor then cooperated with the Oxfordshire County Council in an admirable renovation of the cottages.

Such, then – or something not too much unlike it – was the village to which, at the age of twenty-three, Viscount Falkland returned. Could he now stand on the perimeter of his estate, he would wonder where on earth he was, but when he saw the church and the stocks and the cottages, he would recognise a scene which one of his own poems had praised, saying how restful it is to stroll through the fields:

In June, or when the dog-starre reigns, to find

Some fresher shade, or softer breath of wind,
And taste the spring, whose purer waters drill
From the high top of some exalted hill . . .

So, in the prime of his young manhood, happily married and adequately endowed, Lucius Cary followed a way of life which may in every sense be called the good one.

The best account of those heydays was written by a man who shared them, Edward Hyde, Lord High Chancellor to Charles I and Charles II, and – as Earl of Clarendon – father-in-law of James II. In his famous book, *The True Historical Narrative of the Rebellion and Civil Wars in England*, Clarendon neither hid the defects nor exaggerated the merits of Falkland. First he stated the Viscount's prowess as a scholar in an age when almost every gentleman possessed at least a smattering of Latin, could play a musical instrument, and was a swordsman and a horseman, following the example of Sir Philip Sidney, who confessed that his own Muse

Tempers her words to trampling horses' feet
More oft than to a chamber-melody . . .

Clarendon remarked that Falkland had already 'made himself master of the Greek tongue (in the Latin he was well versed . . .) and had read not only all the Greek historians, but Homer likewise, and such of the poets as were worthy to be perused . . . truly his conversation was one continued *convivium philosophicum* or *convivium theologicum* . . .' Reading made Falkland a full man, but never a pedantic one, for he leavened his learning with 'wit, good humour and pleasantness of discourse, which made the gravity of the argument (whatever it was) very delectable'.

Since it lay within a dozen miles of Oxford, Great Tew attracted eminent guests. Clarendon, indeed, likened Falkland's house to 'the university itself, by the company always to be found there'. Among that company was Gilbert Sheldon, sometime Archbishop of Canterbury; John Earle, Bishop of Salisbury and tutor to the Prince of Wales, who told Clarendon that he had acquired 'more useful learning' at Great Tew than at Oxford itself; and William Chillingworth, Chancellor of the diocese of Salisbury, who was especially welcomed because, having submitted to Rome, he returned to the English fold and wrote *The Religion of the Protestants a Safe Way to Salvation* , which echoed Falkland's loyalty to the English Church. But donnish divines were not the only guests of a host who 'seemed to have his estate in trust, for all worthy persons, who stood in want of supplies and encouragement, as Ben Jonson, and many others at that time . . . ' Falkland neither raised himself on the fame of his guests nor required them to bow to his own rank. According to Ben Jonson, the hospitality at Great Tew symbolised

> Simple love of greatness and of good,
> That knits brave minds and manners more than blood.

Jonson's opinion was shared by Clarendon, who said that Falkland's 'bounties were so generously distributed, and so much without vanity and ostentation, that . . . he did all he could, that the persons themselves who received them should not know from what fountain they flowed . . .' The Manor House, in fact, became a Liberty Hall where poets mingled with prelates: 'Nor,' said Clarendon, 'did the lord of the house know of their coming and going, nor who were in his house, till he came to dinner, or supper . . . there was no troublesome ceremony or constraint, to forbid men to come to his house, or to make them weary of staying there; so that many came thither to study in a better air, finding all the books they could desire in his library, and all the persons together, whose company they could wish, and not find in any other society.' That brand of cultured hospitality continued in England until World War II, whereafter very few major artists and scholars needed to solicit, and very few private gentlemen could afford to supply, board and lodging and books, It is not surprising that, when Falkland undertook a diplomatic mission to Scotland, Abraham Cowley expressed the national concern:

> Great is thy charge, O North! be wise and just,
> England commits her Falkland to thy trust;
> Return him safe; learning would rather choose
> Her Bodley and her Vatican to lose . . .

Falkland himself stated the matter more modestly when he cited the frivolous people who have no inner resources: 'I pity the unlearned gentleman, on a rainy day.'

Lest his own panegyric should be impugned, Clarendon admitted that Falkland was 'smaller than most men; his motion not graceful, and his aspect far from inviting . . . and his voice the worst of all three . . .' Second impressions however, proved that appearances may deceive, for Falkland's small stature 'was quickly found to contain a great heart, a courage so keen, and a nature so fearless, that no composition of the strongest limbs, and most harmonious and proportioned presence and strength, ever more disposed any man to the greatest enterprise'. Lady Falkland certainly saw nothing amiss in him, nor he in her, of whom he wrote:

> O how thy worth with manners may I sing,
> When thou art all the better part of me?
> What can mine own praise to mine own self bring?
> And what isn't but mine own, when I praise thee?

Meanwhile, the storm was gathering that would sweep Falkland away from domestic happiness, into the turmoil of national politics. He had been born during the reign of James Stuart who, as James VI of Scotland, succeeded Queen Elizabeth I on the English throne, accompanied by a retinue of needy and unpopular Scottish nobles. Unlike his great predecessor, the new King – a stranger to the English people – was neither willing nor able to handle the House of Commons adroitly. Instead, he asserted the divine right of kings to govern as they pleased, without interference by any earthly authority. Of his successor, Charles I, a true likeness was painted by Clarendon: 'He was the worthiest gentleman, the best master, the best friend, the best father, and the best Christian, that the age in which he lived produced. And if he were not the best King . . . no other prince was ever unhappy who was possessed of half his virtues and endowments, and so much without any kind of vice.' Unfortunately, Charles had inherited his father's belief in the divine right of kings, and was prepared to deal less than honestly with those who challenged that right. Therein lay the root of a rebellion which many generations of schoolboys have regarded as a romantic duel between Cavaliers and Roundheads; nor is the romanticism confined to children. On one side a Society exists which depicts King Charles as less fallible than he was; on the other side an Association exists which depicts Oliver Cromwell as what he was conspicuously not: a defender of the liberties of Englishmen. Coleridge, a royalist, deplored such romanticism: 'How many books are still written and published about Charles the First and his times! . . . not one of these authors seems able to throw himself back into that age; and if they did, there would be less praise and less blame on both sides.' Falkland, for his part, bestowed the praise and the blame justly, for his knowledge of history told him that violent rebellion usually begets a regime more despotic than the one which it has overthrown. The clouds, however, gathered slowly, seeming to forestall a squall rather than a hurricane. The men who scanned the political sky from Great Tew probably believed and undoubtedly hoped that a compromise would avert a fatal clash between the King and those who wished to increase their own power by curtailing his. To portray the struggle as a popular uprising is absurd. In 1642 not one of the leading rebels wished to upset the existing social order. Levellers or Socialists were no friends to Cromwell, who put them down whenever they threatened his military dictatorship. Servants tended to follow their master, so that a loyal squire enlisted with his men on the Cavalier side, while a disloyal squire led his men to the Roundheads. The House of Commons first lit the fuse by withholding the revenues without which the kingdom could not be governed. As a result, the King was forced to stretch the spirit, and at times to breach the letter, of the law. It is possible that moderate men on both sides might have achieved a compromise which the King would have accepted and honoured, either willingly or under duress; but men who stand in the middle of the road are often trampled down by the extremists on both sides. In any event, when authority yields an inch, it soon finds itself ordered to yield a yard, and then a furlong, and then a mile. Mirabeau and Kerensky paved the way for Bonaparte and Stalin.

When the breach between King and Commons became ominous, Falkland decided that he must quit Great Tew in order to take a more active part in the struggle. At no time was he a sycophant. He opposed the King's excessive levying of Ship Money; he resented Laud's aggressive Anglicanism; he voted for Strafford's trial. Thus far he was prepared to go; but, like Luther, no further. Knowing that Falkland was widely esteemed, the King invited him to become Secretary of State. Falkland at first declined, feeling himself unfitted to cope with the malicious quips, the ignorant howls, the devious stratagems, and the downright dirtiness of many politicians. In the end, however, he was persuaded to change his mind lest a refusal should impair the King's cause; so, while still in his early thirties, the scholar of Great Tew accepted one of the highest offices in the realm. Had the King been more strongly influenced by the advice of Falkland and his friend, Nicholas Culpepper, it is possible that war could have been averted, even at that late hour, for neither Pym nor Cromwell had yet taken complete control of the Commons. Falkland's own political career, though brief, was marked by moderation. Unlike Sir Francis Walsingham, who had spun a web of Tudor spies, Falkland refused to employ men who, as he put it, 'by communication of guilt, or dissimulation of manners, wound themselves into such trusts and secrets, as enable them to make discoveries for the benefit of the state . . .' Likewise he refused to allow 'the opening of letters, upon a suspicion that they might contain some matter of dangerous consequence'. That such forbearance is noble, few will deny; that it offers the best defence against traitors, only a lunatic will affirm. Falkland, at all events, still hoped that a concordat would allow him to return to his wife and his books and his fields; and he hoped even when war broke out in 1642, though by that time the hope was fading. Said Clarendon: 'From the entrance into this unnatural war, his natural cheerfulness and vivacity grew clouded, and a kind of sadness and dejection of spirit stole over him which he had never been used to . . .' During that same year he took precautions against the future: 'In the name of God Amen. I Sr. Lucius Carie KT. Viscount of Falkland . . . concerning my personall estate whereof I shall dye possessed I doe hereby give and bequeathe the same unto my dearly beloved wife Lettice viscountess of ffalkland . . .' Even when the two armies confronted each other, he continued to hope that a single decisive battle would allow both sides to achieve some of their demands, and neither to relinquish too much. Scorning to seek safety in his position as Secretary of State, Falkland fought at Edgehill, the first major encounter of the war, where he further risked his life by trying to save the fugitive rebels. 'When the enemy was routed,' said Clarendon, 'he was like to have incurred great peril, by interposing to save those who had thrown away their arms . . .' When the battle ended inconclusively, Falkland lost all hope, distressed as much by the sight of a nation at war with itself as by the tyranny that would ensue if the royalists were routed. Wilting under the strain, his courtesy gave way to moods of surliness. He neglected his clothes and his person. Clarendon witnessed the change, saying that Falkland lapsed into frequent silences and would suddenly 'with a shrill and sad accent, ingeminate the word *Peace*, *Peace*; and would passionately profess, 'that the very agony of the war, and the view of the calamities and desolation the kingdom did and must endure, took his sleep from him, and would shortly break his heart'. Several months later, while serving at the siege of Gloucester, he expressed a death-wish by taking such unnecessary risks that his friends protested. He was soon to place himself in even greater danger.

During the autumn of 1643 a strong detachment of rebels set out from Swindon to London, hoping to reinforce the City. Prince Rupert, the King's nephew, at once intercepted the march by entering Newbury. Less than three hours later the rebels arrived, seeking food and shelter. Finding themselves forestalled, they retreated to Enborn, a few miles south-west of Newbury. Rupert then held a council of war, at which, forsaking his usual impetuosity, he advised against an immediate attack, arguing that his own troops were awaiting supplies of ammunition from Oxford, and that the rebels were unlikely to move until they had obtained adequate food. His wisdom was out-voted. Next morning, therefore, he led the Royalists to the high ground on Wash Common, very near to Enborn. The rebels attacked immediately. Falkland was ready (he told his friends that he wished to be 'out of it 'ere night'). As though resolved to find at Newbury the release which had eluded him at Gloucester, he dressed in his finest clothes, received the Sacrament from a chaplain, and joined the front rank of Loyd Byron's cavalry. This time he did not fail. A musket ball killed him. His body was found next day, and buried at Great Tew, in a grave that cannot be identified, having been left unmarked lest the Puritan rebels should desecrate it. An entry in the church register states: 'The 23rd day of September, the Right Honble. Sir Lucius Cary, Knight, Lord Viscount of Falkland and Lord of the Manor of Great Tew was buried here 1643.' The nobility of Falkland's character, and the sincerity of his motives, are beyond dispute; his resolution, on the other hand, has been questioned. It is true that he was overwhelmed by events which other men were able to withstand; true also that he sought death in battle; but to accuse him of irresolution is absurd. He need never have entered politics. He need never have fought a battle. By paying his taxes and by keeping his mouth shut he could have joined the considerable number of Royalists who emerged relatively unscathed. But he did enter politics and he did fight a battle. Having used his best talents to avert a war, he fell in the thick of it.

Lady Falkland continued to reside at Great Tew. Her chaplain, John Duncon, revealed that during the early months of bereavement she, too, had wished to die; but she quickly rallied. Despite the reprisals which the rebels were exacting – fines, sequestrations, imprisonment, death – she remained loyal, though never bigoted. To the Cavaliers who protested when she gave shelter to wounded rebels, she replied: 'No one will suspect my loyalty because I relieve these prisoners . . . I would rather thus be misunderstood than that any of my enemies should perish.' She gave true meaning to the Church's holy days, assuring her servants that at such times they were free to cultivate their own severals or allotments: 'These days,' she said, 'are yours . . . and I will not be so unjust as to encroach upon your severals byexpecting any work from you.' According to Duncon, 'much of her estate was yearly given to charity . . . and some of her neighbours, who were very old and not able to work, or very young and not fit for work, were wholly maintained by her; to other poor children she contributed much, both for their spiritual and temporal wellbeing, by creating a Schoole for them . . .'. Besides standing *in loco matris* to the district, Lady Falkland maintained the manor's tradition of scholarship: 'That delight,' she wrote, 'I take in the study of Historie and Philosophie.'

As Falkland had predicted, the rebellion ended in a military dictatorship. Styling himself 'His Highness the Lord Protector', Cromwell would have become 'His Majesty King Oliver' had not the military junta compelled him to change his mind. A member of the Army Council risked death by declaring: 'There is now no visible Authority in the Kingdom but the power and force of the sword.' Cromwell eventually placed the country under martial law administered by eleven so-called Major Generals who ensured that only Cromwell's supporters were returned to Parliament. He imposed the death penalty on anyone who wrote or even spoke unfavourably of his dictatorship. Before long he became so unpopular that he went in fear of his life, and took to changing bedrooms during the night lest an assassin had entered the palace. The Venetian ambassador reported: 'Cromwell is the most hated man in the kingdom.' Puritanism threatened all who would not conform with its own fanatical nonconformity. The Church of England was abolished, the Book of Common Prayer was outlawed. Defying the rebels, Lady Falkland ordered Duncon to read a daily service from the Liturgy. Less than three years later the church register stated: 'The Right Honble. Lettice, Viscountess of

Falkland was buried at Great Tew the 29th day of February 1646.' One of her grandsons, Anthony Cary, became Treasurer and Paymaster of the Navy under James II, and a Privy Councillor under William III; but his career was brief. On 13th May 1698, John Evelyn noted: 'Lord Falkland (grandson of the learned Lord Falkland, Secretary of State to K. Charles and slain in his service) died now of the small pox. He was a brisk, understanding, industrious young man . . . and advancing at the new Court. All now gone in a moment, and I think the title is extinct.'

Lucius Cary, however, is in some ways not extinct, nor is his friend Edward Hyde, for they shine together, like twin stars, in the requiem which the Earl composed for the Viscount: 'Thus fell that incomparable young man, in the four and thirtieth year of his age, having so much despatched the business of life, that the oldest rarely attain to that immense knowledge, and the youngest enter not into the world with more innocence: whoever leads such a life, needs not care upon how short a warning it be taken from him.'

14
Away from it All: Shropshire

When his father was about to retire as the Unitarian minister at Wem, young Hazlitt met the new incumbent, Samuel Taylor Coleridge, who so abmired the Shropshire landscape that he proposed, in Hazlitt's words, 'to write a Sonnet to the Road between Wem and Shrewsbury, and immortalise every step of it'. Rightly or wrongly, however, Hazlitt believed that a man's character can be judged by studying his nose, which Hazlitt himself regarded as 'the index of the will', adding that Coleridge's nose was 'small, feeble, a nothing, like what he has done'. That seems a harsh judgement on *The Ancient Mariner*, yet it was certainly true of the Shropshire sonnet, which Coleridge never did write, pleading that he 'lacked the quaint

Muse of Sir Philip Sidney'.

Were Coleridge alive today he might offer a more convincing excuse, because the road between Wem and Shrewsbury is deafened and polluted by traffic. I once walked on that road, all the way from Wem to Church Stretton, not for pleasure but in order to fulfil a topographical task; and while I walked I wondered for how much longer I could endure the dangerous din. My spaniel, being unaccustomed to those symptoms of Progress, literally dogged my footsteps, wincing whenever a lorry roared within a few feet of us. South of Shrewsbury he took to sitting in the verge, as though begging me to leave the lethal racetrack. After about a dozen miles I complied, exhausted and unnerved. The map showed that I was only a mile or so from a Roman road, Watling Street West, an offshoot from the Roman highway between Dover and Wroxeter. By crossing a few fields I reached the road, a grass track, out of sight and sound of the traffic. There at last I heard the April birds in a land where, as Mary Webb said, 'the dignity and beauty of ancient things lingers long . . .' John Masefield, who was born and bred in Herefordshire, shared Mary Webb's love of Shropshire:

> And looking at that Shropshire scene I cried:
> 'No sunset sees a lovelier countryside . . .'

Within a few minutes my spirits revived and the dog ranged. A second glance at the map showed that the rest of the journey could be made either on the track or close beside it.

The prospect of continuing on Watling Street West recalled memories of Wroxeter, the imperial Uricon or Virocon, an important outpost guarding the Welsh border, still retaining some of its massive sandstone walls. Visitors to the site are not numerous enought to invalidate Mary Webb's Ichabod:

> Where trumpets rang and men marched by
> None passes by the dragon-fly.
> Athwart the grassy town, forlorn,
> The lone down-beetle blows his horn.

The Romans saw Britain as an *Ultima Thule* or end of the civilised world. Soldiers serving on Hadrian's Wall and further north in Perthshire cursed the British climate, and Tacitus supposed that the whole of Britain was permanently shrouded in mist. During my own journey I did notice that the temperature had dropped and that the white clouds were turning grey. I therefore cut short my lunch, scattered the crumbs for the birds, whistled the ranging dog, and followed the green road southward. Away on the right, nearly seventeen hundred feet above sea level, the Longmynd marked the summit of an extensive highland between England and Wales; at its foot lay the little town of Church Stretton, the place beside a *straet* or Roman road, There Mary Webb spend her honeymoon (in her novels the town was called Shepwardine), and from it a number of paths and tracks traverse the bare hills.

A few miles beyond Church Stretton I heard the traffic again. Soon I had to join the main road at Craven Arms, but was able to leave it almost at once, taking a lane to Leintwardine. On that lane the first snowflake fell, so I sheltered under a bridge, watching the lane grow gradually white; and while sheltering I heard the first cuckoo in spring, calling through the snow. No doubt a Roman soldier, dreaming of Italy or Provence, had witnessed the same unseasonable sight; no doubt, like myself, he had hardly finished complaining before the snow ceased, the clouds parted, and the sun thawed the white shroud, leaving the land to glow green again, and the cuckoo to sound less mocking.

The Longmynd lay astern now, but on the left the fields climbed to a wooded skyline, and the lane itself proceeded through an almost uninhabited countryside. Mediaeval Shropshire contained large areas of woodland, whence the magpie or black-and-white houses. Another distinctive feature is the number of Welsh place-names in the county: Bettws-y-Cryn, Llanvair Waterdine, Llanymynech, Myndtown. Buildwas and Offa's Dyke, symbolising a border which Masefield described in 1967: 'The English of the border did not approve of the Welsh; and the Welsh returned the prejudice. The feeling was shared by young and old; the young caught the infection without knowing that it was an infection.'

Many readers of *A Shropshire Lad* assume that Masefield's contemporary, A. E. Housman, was a Salopian by birth; in fact, he was born at Fockbury in Worcestershire, and spent most of his life either in London or in Cambridge. Why, then, did he place his melancholy Lad in Shropshire? Housman answered that question honestly: 'I had a sentimental feeling for Shropshire because its hills were our western horizon.'

Under the lane, or somewhere nearby, lay the paved Roman road, Watling Street West. This was the Shropshire that Mary Webb enshrined in her poetry and novels, likening it to Heaven:

> Ah, haunted were the hills of Heaven,
> Where no tree falls and none is riven,
> Where the frail valley-lilies stay
> Becalmed in beauty, every leaf
> And every flower!

I do not recall seeing a house for several miles. I am certain that no one passed me. Large tracts of Shropshire have escaped over-population. People still keep an ancient toast: 'To all friends round the Wrekin.'

15
The Happiest Man on Earth: Berkshire

Some people and some places seem to have been made for each other. It is difficult to think of Wordsworth apart from Lakeland, or of Emily Brontë apart from Haworth, or of Dr. Johnson apart from London. Granted, Johnson did visit Scotland, and Wordsworth and Emily Brontë did visit the Continent; but their excursions were relatively brief, and in the end they strengthened the travellers' allegiance to their own homes. Although it never became so intense as those earlier affinities, the bond between Yattendon and Robert Bridges was very strong, for the place and the poet shared something of each other's nature. His friend Edward Thompson, Fellow of Oriel College, remarked, Yattendon was 'the deliberate choice of the eye which in all England was the best trained to appreciate our southern landscape'.

Yattendon is a small village, seven miles from the Thames at Pangbourne. My favourite approach begins at Upper Basildon, near the site of a farm that was cultivated by Jethro Tull, an eighteenth-century landowner, whose skill as an inventor of agricultural implements failed to receive the acclaim which it deserved. Tull, in short, was not a happy man. Bridges, on the other hand, *was* a happy man; in fact, he claimed to be the happiest on earth:

> For a happier lot
> Than God giveth me
> It never hath been
> Nor ever shall be.

Born in 1844 at Walmer in Kent, Robert Seymour Bridges came of a line which he described as a 'long-lived aristocracy of generals, baronets, and divines . . . ' He went to Eton and enjoyed every moment of it. In old age he looked back *con amore* when he told the Eton boys:

> Here is eternal spring: for you
> The very stars of heaven are new;
> And aged Fame again is born
> Fresh as the peeping flowers of morn.

It was on just such a morning that I reached the lane from Basildon to Yattendon, climbing among woods where bluebells wove a sky-blue haze. The gentle hills and the thatched cottages tallied with Miss Mitford's temperate eulogy: 'Shady yet sunny Berkshire,' she wrote, 'where the scenery, without ever rising into grandeur or breaking into wildness, is so peaceful, so cheerful, so varied, so English.' The last three of those adjectives can be applied to Bridges himself. At Corpus Christi College, Oxford, he stroked the college boat to second place on the river, and stroked it again at an international regatta in Paris. No other poet – not even Milton – so patiently prepared himself for his vocation. He resolved to be a celibate scientist until he was forty, whereafter he would embrace matrimony and poetry; and that is what he did. Having served for fifteen years as a physician at several London hospitals, he retired, chiefly in order to recuperate from the only illness he ever suffered until the last. In his fortieth year he married Monica, daughter of an eminent architect, Alfred Waterhouse, who lived at Yattendon. During one of my visits to the village I was admitted into the house where the Waterhouse children had grown up; and there, on a wall, I saw the markings that recorded Monica's progress in stature.

The lane to Yattendon is in no hurry to arrive. It twists and climbs through a wooded landscape whose dearth of relevant signposts makes it difficult for a stranger to choose aright from among the anonymous crossroads. In a letter to Bridges, his friend and fellow-poet, G. M. Hopkins, remarked on 'the leagues and parasangs of country lanes' that led to 'a remote world's-end place like Yattendon'. Edward Thompson, Fellow of Oriel College, Oxford, who knew Bridges for many years, did not exaggerate when he said that the hills near Yattendon 'unite stretching vastness with the intimacy and unguarded beauty of woodland coppice . . .'

On the outskirts of Yattendon the lane tries to straighten itself before reaching the parish church, a small yet impressive building, founded by John Norreys, Master of the Wardrobes to King Henry VI. A churchyard Cross marks Bridges's grave. Inside the church, I failed to find a copy of *The Yattendon Hymnal* which Bridges helped to compile as an antidote to the banalities of *Hymns Ancient and Modern*. In an autobiographical fragment, *Letter to a Musician on English Prosody*, he mentioned his musical activities at Yattendon: 'I was once induced to establish a quire in a country church, and among my first tasks I had to train the boys in choral monotone.' Yattendon to-day prefers *Hymns Ancient and Modern*.

Beyond the church, the lane bears left and right, passing several red-brick cottages in spick-and-span gardens. Soon the lane widens a little, flanked by period houses, an old inn (now a hotel), and one or two genteel-looking shops; and there the village ends, not greatly changed since F. L. Griggs described it in 1906: 'comfortable, prosperous, and tidy . . . The roses on the cottages were carefully tended and trained.' In short, Yattendon resembles Bridges himself, being handsome, well-bred, somewhat aloof, yet sociable to its own society; the ideal setting for a man whom the President of Magdalen classified as 'poet, scientist, philosopher, naturalist, musician, philologist, typographer, and country gentleman . . . ' Edward Thompson agreed, seeing Yattendon as 'exactly that ordered world which pleased him in nature and in man's affairs. The machine age had not yet created the internal combustion engine, to shatter the quietness and to set time racing. It was an easy leisured journey to Oxford, whose Common Rooms ensured a continuity of Eton and other friends, now settled in the same security of cultured profession and gracious circumstances as Bridges himself.'

Bridges and his family lived at Yattendon Manor, which soon became a latter-day Great Tew, visited by distinguished poets and scholars. Sir Henry Newbolt loved both the house and the village: 'The charm of that place and that house, for me, could never be expressed, much less exaggerated. The pleasant old red-brick house with its rock-haunted garden had just the combination of beauty, simplicity, and remoteness suitable to a poet of his Miltonic order.' Bridges remained at Yattendon for nearly a quarter of a century, all the while studying prosody, devising new metres, reviving old ones; a labour of love made possible by a private income and an unfeigned disregard of all save a few percipient critics:

> I will be what God made me, nor protest
> Against the bent of genius in my time,
> That science of my friends robs all the best,
> While I love beauty, and was born to rhyme.

Edward Thompson summed it up by saying that Bridges 'was able to live only for the poetry to which he had dedicated himself so long ago'.

At Yattendon, then, in deep contentment with his wife and children, he wrote some of the most beautiful lyrics in our literature. A. E. Housman rated Bridges's first collection as 'the most perfect book of verse ever written'. Edward Thomas told W. H. Hudson: 'I would as soon read his best lyrics as Campion's . . .' Bridges was indeed a *sursum corda* man:

> O happy life! I hear thee sing.
> O rare delight of mortal stuff!
> I praise my days for all they bring,
> Yet only are they not enough.

Again:

> My spirit sang all day
> O my joy,
> Nothing my tongue could say,
> Only my joy!

And again:

> And every eve I say,
> Noting my step in bliss,
> That I have known no day
> In all my life like this.

And yet again:

> Among the meadows
> Lightly going,
> With worship and joy
> My heart overflowing.

Finally, to his wife:

> All my joys my hope excel,
> All my work hath prospered well,
> All my songs have happy been,
> O my love, my life, my queen.

This joy, surely unparalleled in literature, was not caused solely by a private income that enabled him to fulfil his true vocation; it was a genetic gift, revealing what the Warden of New College called 'the normality, the simplicity, the sanity of his nature'. Such a man, and therefore such an art, finds little favour among those who nowadays set Mahler above Bruckner, and Samuel Beckett above J. M. Synge. One may envy Bridges's attitude to life, or one may deplore it; but only the avant-garde will deny that almost everything he published is flawless and felicitous:

> I love all beauteous things,
> I seek and adore them;
> God hath no better praise,
> And man in his hasty days
> Is honoured for them.

A recent survey of English literature, written by A. C. Ward, labelled Bridges as 'a contemplative Oxford recluse', which seems a strange description of a doctor in a slum hospital, a traveller through Europe and America, a parish councillor, a village choirmaster, a host who entertained scores of eminent contemporaries. One wonders whether the poetasters ever read what Bridges wrote, for his joy had sometimes to conquer despair:

> Ah, little at best can all our hopes avail us
> To life the sorrow, or cheer us, when in the dark,
> Unwilling, alone we embark,
> And the things we have seen and have known and heard of,
> fail us.

Along the lanes at Yattendon, or beside the Thames near Mapledurham, you will find some of the scenes which Bridges set to music:

> There is a hill beside the silver Thames,
> Shady with birch and beech and odorous pine . . .

And:

High from his load a woodman pitched
His faggots on the stack:
Knee-deep in straw the cattle twitched
Sweet hay from crib and rack . . .

At a time of life when most other poets are either dumb or dead, Bridges moved from Yattendon to Boar's Hill, within an easy walk of his beloved Oxford; and there he entered on an old age whose serenity matched the fervour of his youth. Truly his work prospered, and the joys multiplied. The children became a source of proud happiness (the son was to receive a peerage for services as secretary to the Cabinet), and his own vigour seemed inexhaustible. When he was past seventy he waded across the Isis rather than await a tardy ferryman. When he was past eighty he declined an anaesthetic during a tooth extraction. At eight-three he was seen to run up and down the stairs at the Oxford University Press. 'He was,' said the President of Magdalen, 'of noble and even heroic presence, and his careless outdoor strength and grace, growing more picturesque with age, expressed the colour and delicacy – as well as the masculine humour and outspoken freedom of his mind.' The gods do not always grant an early death to those whom they love; like Aeneas, Bridges was *hominum divomque voluptas*, blessed with health, happiness and longevity.

He had begun as a lyricist for the few, and in his prime he concerned himself with modes and matters that were unlikely to attract wide notice; yet his light ultimately pierced the bushel which he sometimes placed over it. He received the Order of Merit and the Laureateship of England. On his eighty-fifth birthday the Oxford University Press published his long poem, *The Testament of Beauty*, enshrining a lifetime's meditation on science, religion, philosophy, sociology, ethics, politics, art; written in a metre of his own devising; omega contemplating alpha and the intervening years:

'Twas late in my long journey, when I had climbed to where
the path was narrowing and the company few,
a glow of childlike wonder enthral'd me as if my sense

had come to a new birth purified, my mind enrapt
re-awakening to a fresh initiation of life . . .

Of all other artists, only Verdi achieved a comparable masterpiece at a comparable age. When, under the direction of Sir Humphrey Milford, the Oxford University Press sold 27,000 copies of the collected poems, Bridges – who had for so long disregarded popular acclaim – opened his heart to those whose hearts he had himself opened: 'Milford,' he cried, 'you've made me Laureate!'

He died as he had lived, easily and bravely. Edward Thompson, from whom he differed politically and theologically, paid a tribute which does honour to both men: 'It is not easy to convey to those who never knew him the affection and respect which every thought of Robert Bridges recalls.'

How pleasant it would be to report that at Yattendon the best aspects of Bridges's era merge quietly with the best aspects of our own. Alas, they do not, for Yattendon lies only a mile or so from a motorway, and is harried day and night by aircraft. I lately walked through moonlight there, and with me went a ceaseless rumble from the motorway, drowned briefly whenever an aircraft thundered overhead. The banes of Progress have destroyed the boons of quietude which the English countryside bestowed on Robert Bridges throughout the length of all his days:

I have lain in the sun
I have toil'd as I might
I have thought as I would
And now it is night.

What good have I wrought?
I laugh to have learned
That joy cannot come
Unless it be earned:

For a happier lot
That God giveth me
It never hath been
Nor ever shall be.

16
A Glittering Prospect: Carmarthenshire

Granted a life which spanned several thousand years, we might, if we so desired, explore every lane in Britain. Since we are granted only one life, which seldom spans more than eighty years, we must forego such far-ranging safaris. Nonetheless, having many times passed a lane without following it, we may at last take the plunge, finding that it has led us into Arcady: which was what happened when I set out from Tregaron, intending to follow part of a Roman road, Sarn Helen East, between Llanfair Clydogau and Pumpsaint in Carmarthenshire or *Sir Gaerfryddin*, the largest of all the ancient Welsh counties, set at a safe distance from industrial zones. The mediaeval Princes of South Wales held court at Carmarthen, and the Norman Kings made the town a royal borough. Henry

VII, himself a Welshman, allowed the mayor of Carmarthen to be preceded by a sword on ceremonial occasions. The original Tudor weapon still serves that purpose, and a shepherd near Maesllan told me that when Britain goes to war the sword is carried unsheathed. Nor is the country's importance wholly secular, for at Abergwili, two miles from Carmarthen, the mediaeval Bishops of Saint David's built a palace.

On previous journeys from Tregaron to Pumpsaint I had avoided a very steep and narrow lane which the signposts marked as Mountain Road; but on this journey I did follow the lane climbing high above Pont-gwyp, fifteen hundred feet among woods and streams. After much meandering the lane descended to Llanfair Clydogau, a hamlet beside Afon Teifi, on the edge of the Black Forest. That people do live at Llanfair Clydogau I am convinced, for I have seen smoke curling from chimneys, and ponies tethered to gates, and vegetables growing in gardens; but of the people themselves I have never yet been granted a glimpse. Six times I was at Llanfair Clydogau, and six times the inhabitants remained inaudibly invisible.

South of Llanfair Clydogau, the Roman road can be traced near Llandovery; northward it vanishes, though it may have continued so far as *Bremia*, a small fort. During the last quarter of the first century AD most of Wales was dominated by large Roman forts – at Chester and Caerleon, each containing six thousand legionaries. *Bremia* was one of several small forts in isolated places, manned by auxiliaries or second-class soldiers. Covering five acres, and shaped like a playing card, these forts were surrounded by a ditch and rampart, the latter being topped with turrets. The nucleus of each fort was the commanding officer's residence, the staff headquarters, and the granary, all built of stone. Other buildings – barracks, stores, stables, workshops, sick bay – were built of timber. Baths and perhaps a few native shops lay outside the fort.

South of Llanfair Clydogau, the Roman road appears as a lane through forestry plantations in a wild terrain. The post-Roman name of this route, Sarn Helen East, recalls a word and a woman. The word, *sarn*, is Welsh for 'causeway'; the woman, Helen, is a myth whose legend runs thus: during the third century AD a Spanish-born general, Magnus Maximus, tried to make himself Emperor. Five years later he was killed in battle, having ruled Spain, Gaul, and Britain. During those five years his exploits so impressed the Welsh that they co-opted him as one of their own folk heroes. Prompted by a dream, Magnus set out to find his future wife, Helen, whom he expected to meet in Wales. The Welsh, for their part, showed admiration by giving Helen's name to certain Roman roads. According to *The Mabinogion*, an anthology of Welsh fairy tales, Helen admired the Romans' skill as road-builders: 'She wished to make roads from one fort to another across the Isle of Britain. And the roads were made. And for that reason they are called the roads of Helen, and the men of the Isle of Britain would not have made those great roads for anyone save her.' Some scholars believe that *Sarn y Helen* is a corruption of *Sarn y Lleng* or 'Rome's Highway', the work of men who really did know how to build roads.

For several miles the *sarn* is more or less level lane, but when it begins to descend, it comes within a few feet of the edge of a valley on the left, and in that valley, hundreds of feet below, lies a white farmhouse. When I first saw it, on a spring morning, the place and its occupants reminded me of some lines in the mediaeval *Black Book of Carmarthen*:

> Maytime, the fairest season,
> Loud are the birds, green the groves,
> Plough in furrow, oxen under yoke . . .

When I last saw it on an autumn afternoon, the place and its occupants reminded me of some lines by a twentieth-century Welsh poet, R. S. Thomas:

> The pig is a friend, the cattle's breath
> Mingles with me in the still lanes . . .

There are many types of Welshfolk – colliers, quarrymen, factory workers, clerks, civil servants, and so forth – but the most endearing and also the most enduring heirs of *Cymry* are the hill farmers and their wives: singers *in excelsis*, Calvinists by inheritance, swarthy, suspicious, lovers of their national poetry, neither much more nor much less sinful than the rest of mankind, remnants of a proud and mountainous people, men and women who, having milked six cows by hand, watch the cacophonous folly of television.

Still descending, the lane turns due south, thereby avoiding high ground and several streams. The gradient then becomes so steep that, if you are climbing up it, all you can see is the brow of the lane, disappearing leftward on from the edge of a precipice. For the next three miles the lane indulges a series of bends which suggest that it has deviated from Sarn Helen East. On the outskirts of a straggling hamlet, called Farmers, the Roman road loses itself among trees and streams. Despite much searching, I never could find any trace of the original course. Beyond Farmers the lane re-aligns itself as a straight sector, and after two miles it meets the modern road between Lampeter and Llandovery at the village of Pumpsaint (*pimp* or 'five'), so-called because one of the rocks was said to have sheltered five saints during a storm: Gwyn, Gwyno, Gwynnore, Celymin, and Ceitho (whose name survives at Caio, a village in the district).

George Borrow stayed in Pumpsaint, at the Dolau Cothi Arms, collecting material for his *Wild Wales*. He said he would like to settle at Pumpsaint were it not that he must earn a living by writing travelogues. When Edward Thomas reached the Dolau Cothi Arms in 1912 he wrote a dedication of his own travelogue, *The Icknield Way*, addressed to Harry Hooton: 'for I have walked more miles with you than with anyone else except myself'. *The Icknield Way* is the dullest and most dispirited of all Thomas's books, written when he had almost collapsed under the strain of journalism to support his wife and three children. Even the book's dedication is depressive: 'I walk,' Thomas confessed, 'because it is necessary in order . . . to make a living.' His journey along the Icknield Way took ten days, following an amalgam of modern road, ancient lane, and prehistoric track from Cambridgeshire to the West Country. He was defeated before he started: 'This book for you was to have been a country book, but I see that it has turned out to be another of those books made out of books founded on other men's books.' Fortunately, he soon afterwards met a young American poet, Robert Frost, who pointed out – what Thomas himself seems never to have suspected – that the pot-boiling journalist concealed a poet. Within five years the man who had never before written verse was killed in action, bequeathing a legacy of poems that have secured for him the recognition which in life he neither expected nor received. Meantime, at the Pumpsaint inn, he wrote the final sentence of his dedication: 'As this is the bottom of the page, and as ale is better than ink, though no substitute for it, I label this "Dedication", and wish you with me inside the "Dolau Cothi Arms" at Pumpsaint, in Caermarthenshire.' Forty years after those words were written, I went to Pumpsaint, seeking anyone who had met Thomas there. The landlord of the inn knew nothing of such a man; had, in fact, never before heard of him. Veterans who were customers at the inn in 1912 likewise knew nothing of such a man. The only glimmer of light came from a woman who said: 'If he was a poet and a Thomas, then two-to-one he was Welsh.' In fact, his parents were partly Welsh, and his maternal grandfather was Spanish.

The Dolau Cothi Arms stands on the site of a small Roman fort that guarded a gold mine at a place called *Ogfau* or 'Caves', only a short distance from Pumpsaint. First impressions of the mine are disappointing, for you see only a rocky dell and some caves; but further investigation reveals several shafts. The Welsh had worked the mine before the Romans arrived, practising a crude open-cast method. In AD 75 Rome took control, encouraged by the Emperor, who owned all the imperial mineral rights. To start with, the Romans continued the old methods, though far more effectively than the Welsh had done. Water, for example, was diverted to drive the pumps and to cleanse the ore. Covering eleven miles, and regulated by reservoirs and sluices, two aqueducts were cut into the hillside, sometimes through yards of rock. Experts believe that the aqueducts could have carried three million gallons a day. When the shallow workings had been exhausted, the Romans delved deeper into the rock, whereafter they probably leased the mine to a Briton working under their direction. Since such leases were almost identical throughout the Empire, the routine at Dolau Cothi must have been the same as at Vipasca in Spain, whose *lex* or contract stated: 'The price of the mine shall be maintained according to the edict of the Emperor Hadrian, namely, that the tenants who undertake the expense of a mine in which many partners have an interest, shall be entitled to receive from their partners that which was agreed in good faith. The tenants shall sell as profitably as possible any shares in the mine for which they paid the full price to the Treasury.' Rome was indeed the foremost jurist, as well as the foremost civil engineer, of the classical world.

Peering into the mine shafts at Dolau Cothi, one feels that many workers must have been killed or injured despite the terms of the lease: 'All mines shall be adequately propped and supported, and the tenants must repair old materials. No one may damage the props or pillars. The worker . . . must avoid the ditch carrying water from the shaft.' Pilfering was discouraged, especially among slaves: 'If an ore-thief is a slave the Procurator shall beat him and sell him, on the understanding that the thief must be kept permanently in chains, and forbidden to live in a miners' camp.' Nevertheless, the slaves were entitled to take a hot bath gratis, and the lease itself emphasised the importance of Roman hygiene: 'The lessee, his partner or his agent, at the termination of the lease shall hand over in good and serviceable condition the equipment of the Baths and all things which have been assigned to him, except those that were subject to reasonable wear and tear.'

Little is known of Dolau Cothi between the fourth century, when the Romans abandoned it, and the nineteenth century, when the British re-opened it. In 1888 the mine was worked by South Wales Gold Mine Ltd. Six years later it closed. Reopened in 1904 by a man who had mined tin in Cornwall and gold in South Africa, the venture again failed. In 1933 a new company was formed, employing two hundred local people. For a third time the venture failed.

Dolau Cothi is part of a large estate that was given to the

National Trust in 1941 by Mr. H.T.C. Johnes, whose ancestors had held the land since the reign of Henry VII. The gift commemorated a member of the family, Lieutenant-General Sir James Hill-Johnes VC. Today the mine is open to the public. Are the wild cats still there? A few years ago I shared a sandwich with half a dozen hungry kittens, watched by their fierce-looking mother. Since the kittens spurned the bread, but devoured the meat, I concluded that they were accustomed to receiving visitors' tit-bits.

South of the mine, Sarn Helen East continues toward Llandovery, about eight miles away. While trying to trace the route, I entered Cilycwm, a spick-and-span place, displaying a proud sign: Best Kept Village Cilycwm 1969. A retired postman told me that Cilycwm was honoured among Welsh dissenters because its chapel is one of three claimants to be the oldest Wesleyan meeting house in Wales. I have several times walked and driven along Sarn Helen East, and always I have covered most of the way without meeting anyone. My favourite sector begins as a grass track at Aber Bowlan (a farm and a letter-box), where it fords a stream and for several miles crosses a wild country, almost a thousand feet above the sea. The Roman road-builders must have camped somewhere nearby, watched by hostile tribesmen. Like the British soldiers many centuries later, the Romans observed strict rules of defence. First, the surveyors chose a level area, marking a place for the commanding officer's tent and alongside it the staff headquarters. The men's tents were called a *papilo* because they could be folded like a butterfly. Measuring ten feet square, and lined with straw, each tent held ten soldiers. An officer's tent, erected on a box frame, was twice as large as a *papilo*; the commanding officer's was larger still. The entire camp was surrounded by a ditch, three feet wide and three feet deep, the spoil serving as a wall, into which stakes were driven, seven feet high. Such an encampment could be occupied for several weeks while the soldiers – liable at any moment to be attacked – cursed the cook, the climate, the contours, and the centurions.

John Masefield evoked the danger and discomfort when darkness fell,

And the sentry on the ramparts saw the distance dying
In the smoke of distance blue and far,
And heard the curlew calling and the owl replying
As the night came cold with one star.

The poet Horace composed a *Secular Hymn*, beseeching the sun to shine on Rome 'through ages that shall ever grow more auspicious'. Despite his prayer, the Empire declined and fell, as every other empire has done and must do: *Sic transit gloria mundi*. Some of the Roman roads, however, have survived, and Edward Thomas was therefore correct in saying:

Roads go on
While we forget, and are
Forgotten like a star
That shoots and is gone.

17
The Deserted Village: Northumberland

It would be interesting to understand – though we probably never shall – why a relatively trivial incident should linger in the mind long after a deeper experience has grown dim. Scarcely less interesting would be to know why, having several times passed a lane, we suddenly decide to follow it. Something of the sort occurred while I was tracing the course of a Roman road, Dere Street, from York (*Eboracum*) to the three Eildon Hills (*Trimontium*) near Abbotsford, Sir Walter Scott's old home in Selkirkshire. North of Chollerton the present road deviates from Dere Street, but soon rejoins it near a lane which I had passed several times during the course of several years. Without knowing why, I followed that lane, signposted to Thockrington.

Less than an hour later I wrote a brief account of the journey; now, more than twenty years later, I could quote parts of the account verbatim, beginning with my astonishment at finding a bus ticket on an unfenced lane which delved into an infinity of unpopulated hills. I remember passing through a gate, and assuming that the lane was a cul-de-sac, and Thockrington merely a farm. Wherever I looked, I saw only the bare hills and one skylark. More than ever convinced that the lane ended at a farm, I was about to put back when I reached a knoll, just high enough to emphasise the spaciousness of Northumberland, a quasi-regal county, whose industrial zones cover a very small part of the whole. From the hills above Alston in Cumberland to the river at Coldstream in Berwickshire, and from Alnwick westward to Carter Bar, the county is chiefly farmland and forest and moor. At Flodden, even in summer, you may sit beside the lane without hearing or seeing a car all day; on the hills above Alwinton you may walk all day and all the next without meeting another human being.

Happening to glance north-west from the knoll, I was amazed to sight a church astride another knoll; a church, but no village. Knowing that our forefathers never built a parish church miles from the people who would worship in it, I walked to the edge of the ridge, expecting to find a village on lower ground; but I saw only the chimneys of one cottage and one farm above some trees. I remember saying aloud: 'This is absurd. There *must* be a village.' My imperative, however, was confounded; no village appeared; only those two houses and miles of empty pastures.

I walked back to the church, convinced that it would be locked; and again I was confounded; the church was unlocked and in decent condition, with a gabled stone turret reinforced by a buttress of six receding tiers. The font and most of the chancel were Norman. Moreover, instead of following the fashion of displaying appeals for people impoverished and imprisoned and murdered by their own 'freedom' from British rule, the church offered a brief printed biography of itself, as follows: it was built in 1100 by a Norman family, the Umbravilles, one of whom, Richard Umbraville, damaged some property belonging to the Archbishop of York, and was compelled to forfeit the church by way of recompense. Four centuries later, six Thockrington men were ordered 'to fynde an able prest on the proper coste and expense . . . to celebrate divine service . . . and buyld a sufficient stone hus . . . for the defence of the preste and the fermers and their guddes . . . against the Scottes . . . '

At that point I looked up from the printed card because my dog was barking, no doubt at an elusive rabbit. If I had read no further, I might still be wondering why the church stood so far from a village. Fortunately, I did read on: 'The old village lay to the north of the church. In 1847 a returning sailor brought cholera and the population was wiped out. It was never rebuilt.' As I set down the brief history I reflected that, even if cholera had not struck, the village would almost certainly have been depopulated by Matthew Arnold's 'strange disease of modern life' which now employs one machine to do the work of ten farmhands; a fate not foreseen by Goldsmith's 'Deserted Village':

> Princes and lords may flourish, or may fade;
> A breath can make them, as a breath has made;
> But a bold peasantry, a nation's pride,
> When once destroy'd, can never be supplied

However, my surprise did not end there, for in the churchyard I found that Thockrington had achieved fame via a descendant of one of those six men who were ordered to defend themselves against the Scots. The name of that man was Shafto, and his family were first mentioned *c.* 1240. During the early seventeenth century the Shaftos were living at Bravington Hall, a few miles away; but in 1715 they supported the Jacobite rebels and were punished by the loss of their Thockrington manor. The famous member of the family was Robert Shafto, MP for County Durham, whose portrait by Reynolds still hangs in Bravington Hall. One of Robert's neighbours, Sir Henry Belayse of Brancepeth Castle, had a daughter who fell in love with the MP, as the old ballad recounts:

Bobby Shafto's gone to sea,
Silver buckles on his knee;
He'll come back and marry me,
Bonnie Bobby Shafto.

To the tune of *Brave Willy Forster*, that song is still played on the Northumbrian bagpipes.

This sequence of small incidents did not end at Thockrington, for I knew that somewhere in the district I would find a memorial to the Earl of Derwentwater, who, in 1745, joined the Scottish rebels as they marched with the Young Pretender into England, hoping to reach London, to banish the lawful King, and (though some of them denied it) to impose Roman Catholicism on a people who for two centuries had detested what they regarded as an alien and tyrannical creed.

On my way to the memorial I marvelled yet again at the depths and the loftiness of rural Northumberland. G. M. Trevelyan, born and bred in the county, painted a lifelike picture of the Border Region: 'In Northumberland alone, both heaven and earth are seen; we walk all day on long ridges, high enough to give far views of moor and valley, and the sense of solitude above the world below, yet so far distant from each other, and of such height, that we can watch the low skirting clouds . . . It is the land of the far horizons . . . the procession of long primeval ages that is written in tribal mounds and Roman camps and Border towers on the breast of Northumberland.' You will experience this spaciousness on the lane from Otterburn to Bellingham (the Northumbrians call it Bellinjam) and on the high ground at Elsdon, one of whose parsons, living in a peel tower that is still called The Castle, described the scene in winter: 'There is not a single tree or hedge within twelve miles to break the force of the wind; it sweeps down like a deluge from hills capped with everlasting snow, and blasts almost the whole country . . . it began to snow on Sunday night, and the storm has continued ever since.'

Meanwhile, having reached the site of the memorial, I felt almost as puzzled as I had done at Thockrington, because no memorial was to be seen, not though I paced many yards from the supposed site. As at Thockrington, I stood alone in an apparently endless solitude; only the wind spoke, and some distant Cheviots, and a curlew overhead. The landscape, I reflected, had not greatly changed since the county – and, indeed, much of the north of England – was dominated by the Percys, Earls of Northumberland, immortalised by Shakespeare's Harry Hotspur. Although the last of the male Percys died at Turin in 1670, his great-granddaughter, Elizabeth, inherited the vast Percy estates, and married a Yorkshire baronet bearing the respectable but hardly aristocratic name of Smith alias Smithson. Even in Tudor times the Kings and Queens of England had feared the powerful Earls of Northumberland, but the Hanoverian sovereigns, assured of the family's allegiance, felt it would be wise to elevate such staunch allies. In 1750, therefore, having changed his name to Percy, Smithson was created Earl of Northumberland, and in 1766 the earldom became a dukedom. At present the greatest layman in the north of England is Hugh Algernon Percy, His Grace the tenth Duke of Northumberland, heir to titles that sound like a fanfare from the Middle Ages; Knight of the Most Noble Order of the Garter, Earl of Northumberland, Baron Warkworth, Earl Percy, Earl of Beverley, Lord Louvaine, Baron of Alnwick, Lord Lieutenant of the County of Northumberland; on the female line, a descendant of men who once ruled like kings and dared to overrule their sovereign.

Not for the first time that day, I prepared to leave *re infecta*, my mission unfulfilled; and although I held no brief for traitors, I did admire the courage of the traitor whose memorial had been moved from its former place. Derwentwater, at all events, was – very properly – executed; to have pardoned or even to have reprieved him would have encouraged other parties to invade England. Before he died, however, he revealed that he could have saved his life by forsaking his creed: 'Some means have been proposed,' he said, 'for saving my life, which I look upon as inconsistent with honour and conscience, and therefore I reject them; for, with God's assistance, I shall prefer any death to the doing of a base unworthy action . . . '

Returning to the car, I happened to notice a farmhand some way off, to whom I shouted: 'Is there a memorial hereabouts?' The man did not reply, and I supposed that he had never heard of the Roman milestone which someone had erected as Derwentwater's memorial. However, the farmhand suddenly changed course and came toward me. 'Thou'lt find it on yon ridge,' he said, pointing over his shoulder. Back, then, I went, and duly found the stone; not standing where it had been first set, but lying on its side, half-hidden in the grass.

18
A Slough of Despond: Perthshire

Leaving the car beside an empty road, I headed into the moor, squelching through mud, slipping on rocks, head down against a cold drizzle. Ten minutes later I was marooned in the desolation of Rannoch Moor, the most dispiriting region I have ever explored. The Pass of Glen Coe and the heights above Ennerdale Water may appear more fearsome, but they do at least alert the mind, if only by alarming it, whereas Rannoch depresses the mind by numbing it with monotony. The moor covers sixty square miles of a triangle formed by Loch Rannoch, Loch Tummel, and Kingshouse Inn. Only one road crosses it, and only along the western perimeter. The highest point is 1,795 feet; the lowest, 540 feet. A forester at Tyndrum had told me that for a distance of ten miles the contours remain constant at about 950 feet; in other words, the land within that area is as level as the Fens.

In poor visibility I could just see the encircling mountains – Meall Buidhe, Meall Cruinn, A'Crusch – and also a number of trees. According to the Tyndrum forester, trees on Rannoch Moor prefer gradients of not less that 1-in-7 because a lesser incline cannot adequately drain the heavy rainfall. During the Quaternary Glaciation, which ended ten thousand years ago, Rannoch Moor was buried under an ice-sheet many hundreds of feet thick. The native pines are relics of forests that were either felled or burned, partly to provide timber for the Atholl estate and partly to flush out the wolves and brigands sheltering there. In 1579 Sir Donald Monro reported that a certain Highland loch was bounded by a strip of land 'ane myle lange, full of wood, guid for fostering theives and rebellis'. It is said that the last Highland wolf was shot in 1743. When Bishop Leslie of Ross assessed the Highland livestock three centuries ago he mentioned the wild cattle but not the sheep, which suggests that the latter could not elude the marauding wolf-packs. Despite their bleak habitat, the Dukes of Atholl led a lordly life. Defoe said of one eighteenth-century duke: 'The pomp and state in which this noble person lives, is not to be imitated in Great Britain; for he is served like a prince . . . I have been told that he can bring a body of above 6,000 men together in arms at very little warning.' The present duke still maintains a small private army which assembles for peaceable duties on festive occasions.

After three miles I decided that a little of Rannoch Moor went a very long way indeed. The mere act of walking over boulders and bogs was tiring, mentally as well as physically. The silence, which elsewhere would have seemed restful, became oppressive. The only sign of humanity was a distant railway, spanning the moor from Achallender to Rannoch Station. During an earlier journey through Perthshire I decided that Rannoch Station and the small hotel nearby are the most isolated in Britain, for there the road ends after a long and lonely trek beside the northern shore of Loch Rannoch and Loch Tummel. If you walk a few hundred yards beyond the hotel, you enter seemingly infinite wilderness.

At the fifth mile I agreed with the eighteenth-century

traveller who described Rannoch Moor as 'an immense vacuity, with nothing in it to contemplate, unless the numberless misshapen blocks of stone rising hideously above the surface of the earth'. Overhead, the sky was empty of birds, all around, the land was empty of livestock; underfoot, I recognised heather (*Calluna vulgaris*), cross-leaved heath (*Erica tetralix*), and bog moss (*Sphagnum*). Eventually one bird did fly past, too dim to be identified, uttering a wistful cry. Had I proceeded I would have reached one of the small areas of cultivated moorland. Modern farmers can say of Rannoch Moor what Bunyan said of another place: 'It is the Slough of Despond still, and so it will be when they have done what they can.'

At the sixth mile the mist thickened, and the drizzle became a deluge. Forewarned that such things were common, I had taken several bearing en route, and was therefore able to check my position with fair accuracy; so, through silent vagueness, the dog and I returned to the car, still slipping and squelching. Although the journey had been relatively short, the going reminded me of Hilaire Belloc's boast:

> Walked I, went I, paced I, tripped I,
> Marched I, held I, skelped I, slipped I,
> Lingered loitered, limped and crept I,
> Clambered, halted, stepped and leapt I . . .

I reached the car in time to see an elderly man on a bicycle, though whence he had come and whither he was bound altogether baffled me because the road passes very few houses between Tyndrum and Glen Coe, a distance of some thirty miles. The cyclist dismounted, evidently wishing to talk. Without any salutation or preamble, he said: 'On Rannoch Moor they plough up bones.'

'Whose bones?' I asked.

'Men's bones. Irish navvies. They helped to build this road, and some of 'em took so many wee drams they stumbled into yon bog and drowned face-downward in six inches o' slime.'

'It's certainly a wild place,' I agreed.

'And the Irish were certainly a wild lot.' Almost in the same breath he added: 'You've no' surely been walking for pleasure?'

'From curiosity.'

'Isna' that what killed the cat?'

'I have a map and compass.'

'No doubt. But do you ken to use 'em?'

'I can navigate small boats over short distances.'

'Ah.' The Highlander revised his first impressions, but was not wholly reassured. 'People who know the moor,' he said 'gie it a wide bairth in winter. My ain father was buried under the snow, within shouting distance o' Kingshouse. The trouble was, he hadna' the strength to shout.'

'Was he . . . '

'No, he wasna' deed. Not quite. And when they plied him wi' brandy they couldna' stop him from shouting. They say he sang Robbie Burns by heart for half an oor. A wonderful thing is brandy.' The cyclist then mounted his machine, saying: 'I wish you guid day.' At the risk of falling off, he called over his shoulder: 'In the Highlands you've no' to play games wi' the elements.'

Still wishing that I asked the man where he lived and whither he was bound, I drove slowly away, meeting no traffic, seeing only peat and rocks, and knowing that they extended far into the mist, the rain, the solitude, the silence. However, I did find something cheerful to report, for after several miles a solitary house appeared, displaying a signboard. Entering, I was greeted by a young man and his wife, who soon returned with a pot of tea and a plate of scones. While I was paying the bill, the proprietor pressed a small flask of brandy into my hand.

'How kind,' I told him. 'But I seldom drink.' The couple looked so disappointed that I added: 'Nevertheless, I'm most grateful.'

The young man then revealed the reason for his generosity. 'It's a symbolic gift,' he said. 'We've only just started the business, and you're our first customer.'

19
Up the Creek: Cornwall

If you wished to do so, you could probably spend a whole week there without seeing or hearing anyone at all. The only person I ever encountered was a farmer who had climbed down the steep fields. My own journeys thither ought really to be described as voyages because I was then living in a boat. This boat played such a memorable role in my life that I am reluctant to describe the place without saying something of the means by which I reached it. I cannot remember what the boat was called when I first saw her, beached high and dry below Froe Farm on Percuil River, a salt-water creek near St Anthony-in-Roseland in Cornwall. Having bought her, I named her *Noah's Ark*, for that was what she looked like . . . a clinker-built ship's lifeboat, twenty-eight feet long, with a cabin tacked on for'ard, a twelve-horsepower Thorneycroft marine engine, a mast, a wheel, a pump, and very little else. The cabin had a glass windscreen in the bows and ample locker space, but not standing headroom. For economy's sake I replaced the powerful petrol engine with a three-and-a-half horsepower Kelvin engine, primed with petrol and then switched over to paraffin. This gave six or seven knots with wind and water, and steerage way against them. Such, then, was the boat in which I first made a landfall off the beaten track, and the manner of that making was as follows. One summer morning, soon after I had gone to live in *Noah's Ark*, I decided to explore the creek above my anchorage in a wide and beautiful creek near Percuil, surrounded by hills, and in places almost dimpled by trees on the bank. Knowing that the creek's upper reaches dried out at low water, I started while the tide was still making, and as *Noah's Ark* drew only a few feet of water, I felt confident of not going aground. To begin with, the creek remained several hundred yards wide, but after less than a quarter of a mile the hills closed in and the curves became sharper. Proceeding at four knots, I was able to admire the scenery while the fairway delved deeper into the hills. Presently the creek grew so narrow that I wondered whether I would be able to put about. I therefore closed the throttle, just in time. Less than fifty yards ahead, the creek ended at a foot of a steep hill. By spinning the wheel, I managed to bring the boat round; that done, and an anchor dropped, I went below to make coffee.

The next couple of hours were idyllic, serenaded by thrushes, blackbirds, and a cuckoo echoing from shore to shore. On each side the land was so close that, by paying out the dinghy, I enabled the dog to exercise himself in a field. Not often can one enter the heart of the hills while at the same time remaining on salt water. Moreover, to live in a boat, no matter how small she may be, or how near to the shore, is to achieve a respite from what Richard Jefferies called 'the pettiness of house-life – tables and chairs – the pettiness of observances, the petty necessity of useless labour . . . ' In that creek I lingered until the ebbing tide revealed a foot of mud between the boat and the banks. Then the dog was recalled, the anchor came up, and I returned to the deeper waters at Percuil.

After lunch I rowed ashore and climbed the lane toward Gerrans, whence I cut across the fields and looked down on the narrowest part of the creek where only a trickle of water marked the fairway. If *Noah's Ark* ever ran aground there, she would stay immobile and listing for several hours. Once, in fact, she did run aground, but only because I had gone there in order to shelter from a midnight gale that was wrenching boats from their moorings below Percuil.

For several years I made a point of returning to that idyllic creek, which for me held the same attractions as did Helford River for Sir Arthur Quiller-Couch when he sailed there in a boat bigger and more comfortable than *Noah's Ark*. Quiller-Couch remembered those inshore voyages:

> All the woods to ransack,
> All the waves explore –
> Moon on Calamansack,
> Ripple on the shore.

During my own voyages the four seasons offered their various gifts. In September, when I had mastered the business of gauging the tide and the right moment at which to put about, I stepped into a field so covered with mushrooms that I ate little else until the taste cloyed. In December, when much of the rest of Britain was shivering, I lay full-length in the grass, feeling the sun on my face. In April, when lambs bleated and cuckoos called, the primroses were so plentiful and so large that I dug up a few, and later planted them in my garden on the Chiltern Hills, where although they flourished, they dwindled from the size of a florin to the size of a shilling. In August, when the boat's brightwork became almost too hot to touch, I sat in the shade of a tree, away from the stinging insects and a searing sun. It was then, for the first time and the last, that I met someone, a farmer descending the hill. Glancing at *Noah's Ark* and then at the water, he began: 'If 'ee bide there any longer . . . '

'I shan't,' I assured him.

'But if 'ee do . . .'

'The creek will dry out, and I'll have to wait several hours before she rights herself.'

'So 'ee knows?'

'I do now,' I replied.

'Ah. Was it *Noah's Ark* that came yere when the gale . . . '

'It was,' I nodded, once more interrupting his good intentions.

'Then how on earth did 'ee manage to find . . .'

'By God and by guess,' I told him, yet again interrupting, this time by quoting an old sailor's saying.

'It don't seem I can teach 'ee much,' the man smiled.

'I wouldn't say that. But I do think I know this creek and this boat.'

'Her's a queer-looking old tub, if 'ee don't mind me saying so.'

'I don't mind at all. She *is* old, and a tub, and queer-looking, too.'

'But seaworthy, I'd say. A bit low in the gunwale maybe, yet she was built to carry folks across the ocean if need be.' This time he looked at the sky. 'Master warm this morning, eh? If only we'd 'ad a pen'orth o' warmth when they lambs was dropped. But there 'tis. As the good book says, "The Lord giveth, the Lord taketh away".' He scratched his brown nape. 'All the same, there's times I do truly think the Lord don't giveth quite as much as He might . . . not to us farmers, anyway.'

Seeing me go for'ard to raise the anchor, he added: 'So you really do know this creek.'

'Another ten minutes – even five – and I'd be beached.'

'Too true, you would.'

'You don't object if I step ashore sometimes?' I asked.

'Come as often as you please. 'Tis the townsfolk I object to, not that many of 'em come yere. That'd mean walking a bit. But some of 'em light fires, and leave gates open, and scare the sheep, and Lord knows what else.'

Above the sound of the engine, I heard him say: '*Bon*

voyage. Maybe we'll meet again sometime. Oh, by the way, if you do see 'em, remember me to old Perry and 'is missus at Percuil. They'm both a zany, but they mean well, and that covers a multitude o' their nosey-parkings.'

I nodded and waved, feeling sorry to leave such a placid haven, yet glad to know that I would return there, soon and often.

20
The Modern Middle Ages: Nottinghamshire

Laxton is a village which attracts people from many parts of the world. Some of the visitors are ordinary tourists; others are farmers, historians, economists, sociologists, journalists, television producers. Why, then, does this small and secluded place receive such an assortment of sightseers? That question certainly seems hard to answer when you approach Laxton from Newark-on-Trent. After a few miles you leave the loud main road and follow the signposts across undulant farmland. All the lanes to Laxton – from Boughton, from Ossington, from Kneeshall, from Egmanton – are narrow, twisting, and deeply rural. Suddenly, from a hill, you sight the village, and your first impression may be disappointing because all you do see is a cluster of red-brick Victorian houses. These create a pleasant picture, but not a showpiece.

Built on a slope, the main street is flanked by barns and farmhouses, an unusual feature insofar as most other English villages have their farmhouses and barns on the perimeter. Halfway up the hill, you pass the Dovecote Inn, set back from the street. On the summit stands a mediaeval parish church, ineptly restored during the nineteenth century. On the church's north wall you will find details of the priest's glebe as it was in the eighteenth century; and there lies a clue to Laxton's fame, for instead of being a single plot of land, the glebe – like most of the other land in the parish – was a number of widely scattered strips. Laxton, in short retained its mediaeval pattern of husbandry and land tenure long after they had vanished elsewhere in England. Admittedly, England does still contain one or two other traces of the mediaeval pattern, notably near Haxey in Lincolnshire, but only at Laxton is the pattern precise and zealously maintained by the tenants.

If your history is not too rusty, you will recall that William the Conqueror rewarded his principal followers by granting them estates in England. Being himself the turbulent vassal of the French King, the new King of England lessened the threat of rebellion among his own vassals by ensuring that they did not receive huge estates in any one part of the kingdom. The few exceptions to the rule were trusted relatives and friends whom William appointed as vice-regents along the Welsh and Scottish borders. Every principal landowner or tenant-in-chief held his estates in return for military service and general assistance in governing England. In return for lesser services, the tenants-in-chief granted part of their lands to subordinate tenants. Even the lord of a single manor granted land to peasants who tilled his own holdings. This, the so-called feudal system, was a flexible pattern rather than a rigid mould; it had existed before 1066, and in some ways it varied from region to region. Since a peasant's holding was scattered over a wide area of the manor, much time was wasted in moving from strip to strip. However, mediaeval husbandry was relatively primitive, and the people whom it supported were relatively few, so that none needed to own his own out-buildings and farmhouse (the word 'farmhouse' did not appear until 1598). The lord of several manors lived at each of them in turn, and his peasants lived in 'cots' or semi-hovels.

Is Laxton still the home of primitive farmfolk? By no means, for although the village retains its open-field system, it has modernised its methods of farming. This was emphasised by a leading Laxton farmer, John Edmund Rose, who succeeded his father as bailiff of the manorial court which supervises the tillage and imposes a fine on all who break the rules. As I saw for myself, Mr Rose's farm is a model of modern efficiency. Laxton's three great fields, he told me, are South Field, West Field (which is usually kept for spring corn) and Mill Field (the windmill collapsed in 1910). The fields vary in size from 140 to 200 acres. Their strips likewise vary in size, from a quarter-acre to several acres. Crops are so rotated that there is always a wheatfield, a hayfield, and a cornfield. Five centuries ago Laxton's system was the rule, not an exception; but thereafter the system changed, most markedly when sheep became very profitable because of their fleece, and then again when many eighteenth-century estates were enclosed. Most of those enclosures required an Act of Parliament, and the speed at which they increased was remarkable. Between 1702 and 1760 the number of such Acts was about 280, but between 1760 and 1780 the number exceeded 4,000. In the course of eighty years about two million acres were enclosed. By the end of the eighteenth century Laxton's open fields had become such a rarity that a survey for the Board of Agriculture remarked: 'It is a large open-field lordship.'

The Laxton estate still covers some 2,000 acres and includes seven farms whose average size is 100 acres. When I visited the village there were fourteen full-time farmers and about ten or a dozen smallholders. Each of the three great fields is served by stone tracks leading to sykes or areas of unenclosed pasture, covering about eighty acres. In all this the laxton manorial court plays an important role. It meets twice a year, when the bailiff summons farmers by ringing a bell, and anyone who fails to attend is fined twopence. Other fines are imposed for other infringements of the rules. On one occasion the lord of the manor, Earl Manvers, was fined for leaving a load of soil on one of the tracks. The court elects a jury of twelve who allot the strips and decide when the fields shall be opened for grazing. In December the jury inspects the strips to ensure that they have been properly tended. Once again, a fine is imposed on backsliders. Half of the various fines goes to the lord of the manor, the other half provides beer for the jury. Beer and cheese are also supplied by a custom whereby the highest bidder for each syke pays one shilling into the fund, and the refreshment is enjoyed by all the farmers.

There are two main reasons why this unique system of husbandry has survived into the twentieth century: first, because the mediaeval manor was divided among a relatively large number of farmers under a lord who never enclosed it; second, because an *esprit de corps* remains strong in the parish. Indeed, what we now call conservation is probably more influential than ever; consider the church, for example. In 1790 a visitor to Laxton described its condition thus: 'The floor and old stones are completely covered with coals, coal-slack, cinders, fire-wood, straw, lime, broken bricks and stone, hassocks, and flat mats torn in pieces, ladders, an old sieve, broken scuttles and spades, brushes without handles, and handles without brushes, mortar boards and mortar, reeds, tiles, soot, broken glass, dog's dung . . . How has it happened that not one fostering hand has been found in Laxton or its neighbourhood . . . Is it left for the present age to despise, condemn, or neglect these monuments of the pious, the charitable, and the good . . . ?' That doleful Ichabod can be applied to several other aspects of Laxton. The castle decayed four centuries ago; the manor house, three centuries ago. The resident parish priest has gone, the school has gone, and so have all save one of the shops. When I was at Laxton during the early 1980s the prospects for its survival as a unique parish were gloomy, for Earl Manvers had sold the manor to the Ministry of Agriculture in 1951, so that each successive minister was *ex officio* lord of the manor. Mr Rose told me that the government might sell the estate to a person or persons who could know more about profit than about tradition and the wishes of the tenants. Against that, almost everyone in the village, and many people outside it, were resolved to maintain that tradition, even although neither they nor the National Trust could afford to buy Laxton if it were offered for sale. To preserve a way of life solely because it *is* old may be sentimental and unrealistic. No sane man would wish to ressurect surgery without anaesthetics. Laxton, however, is efficient despite its old-fashionedness. Modern farming methods have merged with aspects of mediaeval husbandry and land tenure. The matter was summarised by the late Professor J.D. Chambers, who spent many years studying Laxton and the working of its three fields. 'At present,' he wrote, 'there are seventeen farmers, making a modest living from a system of farming that is utterly obsolete. It is only through their willing co-operation with a generous landlord that it can be preserved for the instruction and delight of its friends and admirers in this and many other countries in the world.'

21
No Man's Land: Roxburghshire

Two roads lead from Carlisle to Hawick. One of them goes via Langholm, the other via Newcastleton. I prefer the latter because it is lonelier and wilder. The first ten miles of the journey are industrial and therefore dreary. Like those in most other British cities, the suburbs of Carlisle tally with Sir Thomas More's *Utopia*: 'He who knows one of the cities, knows them all, so exactly alike are they . . . '

At Longtown, the last village south of the Border, the landscape becomes less dreary and the Scottish hills appear as faint smudges on the sky. In 1698 Celia Fiennes noticed that the Border does not mark a dramatic change of scene. 'I came,' she wrote, 'to Long Town which. . . is called a Border and indeed is very like the Scots land . . . ' Living up to its name, Longtown straggles and would seem ungainly were it not for a spacious street of well-kept houses, designed two centuries ago by Dr. Robert Graham, who lived in Netherby, a few miles away. On the northern edge of Longtown a bridge spans the River Esk, separating England from Scotland; but in Miss Fiennes's day the river lacked a bridge: 'I saw the common people take off their shoes and holding up their clothes wade through . . . this is their constant way of travelling from one place to another . . . they make no use of bridges and have not any.' Half a century later, when the defeated Jacobites arrived, the river still lacked a bridge. One of the rebel officers, the Chevalier de Johnstone, boasted that the fugitives forded the river without losing a man (the only casualties were a few female camp-followers). Two miles beyond Longtown the road passes the site of Scotch Dyke Station, part of a North British Railway network that served the Lowlands from Dumfries to Blyth and from Carlisle to Edinburgh. Scotch Dyke Station stood south of the present roadside Border signs, which are set several hundred yards apart, as though each were anxious not to appear imperialist.

The first Scottish village, two miles beyond the Border, is Canobie, an attractive place, cupped in a valley beside the Esk, This is farming country, not yet rugged, but already undulant. Canobie was one of those Lowland villages whose laziness shocked Celia Fiennes when she found several women sitting idly by the fire at nine o'clock in the morning. Thirty years later *The Statistical Account* reported that Canobie had mended its ways: 'Many circumstances have occurred within these 20 or 30 years to introduce a change in the disposition and manners of the people . . . horse-racing and cock-fighting were much in vogue.' The principal landowner, the Duke of Buccleuch, encouraged Canobie's reformation: 'His Grace has reserved the houses upon the farms in his own power . . . In all new leases a clause of nullity is inserted in case of moral delinquencies therein specified.'

A generation which flies over national frontiers without noticing them may feel that to cross from one country to another is no great matter, least of all when the two countries are nominally one. The Scots, however, differ from the English, for they evolved as a blend of Irish Celts, of Scandinavian pirates, and of migrants from the English Border counties. Scottish law differs from English law; the Scottish Kirk differs from the English Church; the Scottish language likewise differs, though in Roxburghshire less than 0.19 per cent of the people now speak it. Figuratively, therefore, and also physically, Canobie marks a parting of the ways, because there the major road turns east for Langholm while the minor road turns west for Newcastleton, climbing steeply above Liddell Water. Soon the rail-less railway limps alongside, like a ghost seeking its former stations at Riddings, Haithwaite, Kershopefoot, and Newcastleton. How vividly I remember the trains at those small stations, simmering on a summer morning, glowing on a winter night. Wagons came to collect a bull or to deliver a plough. Dog-carts came, delivering parcels or collecting housewives. Always the talk was local: 'I'm away to Caril' . . . 'The wee bairn's hame frae Felstone' . . . 'Angus saw a bonnie coo, but at ten guineas he wouldna' buy' . . .'Near Shankend the drifts were that deep the station master telegraphed for a snow-plough' . . . 'I'd no' care to live at Hawick. I bide here among my ain folk.'

After what seems a very long time indeed, the road enters Newcastleton, a well-bred village, designed as a weaving settlement by the Duke of Buccleuch in 1793. The wayside trees and lawns remind a northbound traveller that he will soon reach bald horizons and swampy hinterlands. Newcastleton, in fact, is so isolated that most of its working inhabitants are either farmhands or foresters. If an urban southron were to walk a few miles beyond the village he might lose his nerve and hurry back, saying that the road had become a lane, dotted with passing-places for vehicles which never appeared; that the hills gave him the creeps; and that the absence of houses seemed unnatural.

Three miles north of Newcastleton the road again bisects itself, the right-hand fork leading to Jedburgh via Bonchester Bridge; the left-hand fork leading to Hawick via nowhere at all. I prefer the latter because it ventures into the heart of Liddesdale. If you follow it for six or seven miles you will reach a lane on the left offering a splendid walk through hills whose highest point, Cauldcleuch Head, is only four feet short of two thousand. On this lane stands Hermitage Castle, so-named because it was built near the site of a hermit's hovel. What you see to-day is a roofless rectangular fortress whose massive sandstone walls rise from a knoll above Hermitage Water. The grassy environs are well maintained by sheep and the Ministry of Works. I doubt that any other Lowland castle occupies a lonelier setting.

Hermitage Castle belonged to the thirteenth-century de Soules, then to the Douglases, and then to the Dacres who captured it for England. During the Middle Ages, however, a Border castle was liable to be re-captured, and Hermitage soon fell into Scottish hands; but the place was of such military importance, and its owner, Archibald Douglas, Earl of Angus, was of such doubtful loyalty, that he was ordered to exchange the castle for a less vital one, Bothwell Castle, on the Clyde. Sir Walter Scott mentioned Archibald Douglas in *Marmion*:

> Princes and favourites grew tame
> And trembled at the homely name
> Of Archibald Bell-the-Cat;
> The same who left the dusky vale
> Of Hermitage in Liddesdale . . .

Archibald's nickname recalls the story of mice wishing that they could tie a bell to the cat's neck and thereby receive warning of the predator's approach. Archibald himself once volunteered to 'bell-the-cat' by waylaying an unpopular courtier.

Hermitage Castle became famous when James Hepburn, Earl of Bothwell and Lord High Admiral of Scotland, rode out to arrest John Elliott, a Liddesdale brigand. Shots were fired, and both men fell; but whereas Bothwell lay wounded, Elliott escaped and set himself to song;

I vanquished the Queen's lieutenant;
And gar'd his fierce troopers flee,
My name is little Jock Elliott,
And wha' daur meddle wi' me?

But Bothwell was more than the Queen's Lieutenant; he was her confidant and probably her lover. Meanwhile, his servants carried him to Hermitage Castle, fearing that he would soon die. Now it so happened that Mary, the French-born Queen of Scots, was then presiding over a Justice Court in Jedburgh, twenty-five miles away. When news of Bothwell's plight reached her, she rode immediately to Hermitage, a journey made dangerous by rough tracks and ruthless robbers. After comforting her lover, she returned to Jedburgh, having ridden fifty miles in one day. On dismounting she collapsed and remained unconscious for several hours. Delirious fever ensued, lasting a week. Finally, she became unconscious again. According to Froude, 'she was supposed to be dead or dying'. The royal physician, a Frenchman, ordered the Queen's arms and legs to be pulled violently. When that failed, the Queen's legs were tightly bound from the toes upward, and wine forced down her throat. Despite the physician, the patient recovered, but the perils of Liddesdale outlived her. On reaching Carlisle, two centuries later, Celia Fiennes 'took a Guide . . . and so went for Scotland . . .' Whenever an Assize Judge crossed the Border into Scotland the tenants of every manor through which he passed provided him with an armed escort. Macaulay was justified in saying: 'No traveller ventured into that country without making his Will.'

Beyond Hermitage the lane twists like a serpent trying to elude the streams descending from left to right: Watt's Burn, Roughly Burn, Whiterope Burn, Laiddlehope Burn, Sundhope Burn, Pittyshield Sike, Black Cleuch. Right and left, too, the hills rise higher? Bell Hill (1,135ft.), Coopercleuch Knowe (1,423 ft.), Lalblair Hill (1,635 ft.), Gratmoor Hill (1,964 ft.). Suddenly the rail-less railway reappears, as though it were still seeking the vanished stations at Steele Road, Riccarton, Shankend. Marooned among such solitude, a modern traveller may marvel that those stations were ever built; in fact, the line linked England with the Lowland tweed manufacturers, calling at stations which served isolated cottages and farms. Having arrived, the railway soon departs, turning north-west while the lane turns north-east. Bereft of that brief ghost, and encircled by empty hills, the traveller feels as Wordsworth did when he climbed Kirkstone Pass, alone in a land

> Where, save for the rugged road, we find
> No appanage of human kind,
> No hint of man . . .

Actually, a hint of man does appear, in the guise of one telephone wire and several small bridges across the multitudinous streams: Leap Burn, Flosh Burn, Langside Burn, Harwood Burn. I have driven and walked along this sector half a dozen times, without meeting either a pedestrian or a vehicle. I once spent three hours at the site of Lime Kiln Edge Station, and still nobody passed. A retired shepherd subsequently told me that in winter the lane may be empty for days.

At Roberts Linn Bridge I always halt, partly to exercise the dog, partly to hear the harmony of wind and water, and partly to confirm that Liddesdale has not greatly changed since Sir Walter Scott first saw it, he being then twenty-six years old and lately called to the Scottish Bar. Although he admired the architecture of his native Edinburgh, he did not at all relish the oppressive Calvinism: 'This being sermon (Sacrament) week,' he wrote, 'we are looking very religious and very sour . . . ' In order to escape from the Kirk's tedious bigotry he acquired a passion for open air life, which in later years led him to belittle the writer's sedentary occupation. To his biographer and son-in-law, John Lockhart, he confessed: 'You know I don't care a curse about what I write, or what becomes of it.' His most memorable escape from Edinburgh occurred when his father sent him to Jedburgh, to seek a brief from the Lord Justice Clerk who was on circuit there. At Jedburgh the fledgling barrister met Robert Shortreed, the Sheriff of Roxburghshire, a braw lad indeed, who told him that Liddesdale abounded not only in Border ballads, many of which he knew by heart, but also in moorland tracks, of which he could say, as Malcolm would one day say in *The Lady of the Lake*:

> As safe to me the mountain way
> At midnight as in blaze of day.

Scott begged Shortreed to take him on safari through the wild and romantic region: so off they went, the Sheriff and the barrister, galloping over the September heather – away from Jedburgh, away from Calvinism – into misty dawns and moonlit nights. Sometimes they slept snugly at a farmhouse; sometimes coldly on a peat-stack. Shortreed remembered his young companion's exultation, and in later years he recounted it to Lockhart: 'Eh me, sic an endless fund of good humour and drollery as he then had wi' him! Never ten yards but we were either laughing or roaring and singing . . . He aye did as the lave did, never made himsell the great man, or took ony airs.' Scott's foray into Liddesdale was probably the most joyful experience in a life which became increasingly sorrowful. During the next seven summers he returned to Liddesdale, once again riding with Shortreed, who summed it up succinctly: 'He was main hisell a' the time but he didna maybe ken what he was about till years had passed.' How true, for the mature artist brought Liddesdale alive in *Guy Mannering* . . . the speech, the silence, the solitude, the stars. It was the gayest book he ever produced, and the writing took less than six weeks.

Near the foot of The Pike the railways makes yet another appearance, keeping close to the lane for about a mile, at which point I always halt again, this time to revisit the derelict station at Lime Kiln Edge. When I last went there, a year ago, the station-master's house was doorless, paneless, and almost roofless. A wind whined among the ruins, as though mourning the desolation that was once a home. Platform and signals had vanished; only the impermanent way remained, covered with grass. People under seventy years of age can only imagine the impact of railways on countryfolk who lived in remote places at a time when cars were seldom seen there. John Bright, the Victorian orator, claimed that 'Railways have rendered more services, and have received less gratitude, than any other institution in the land'. They have certainly done far less harm than have the aircraft and motor vehicles which now foul the air and deafen the ear. On this line the stations enabled passengers to reach Hawick or to visit a relative thirty miles away. Between November and March, when blizzards may obliterate large tracts of Scotland, a train is still the only vehicle that can be confident of reaching its destination north of Carlisle. Moreover, when telephones and daily newspapers were a prerogative of the few, the railway was both a lifeline and a grapevine. News passed from station to station, gathering mass with momentum. On the few branch lines that still do ply, the driver or the guard will give local news to the signalman or the porter, who in turn may add their own contributions.

A cottage stands near the derelict station at Lime Kiln Edge, miles from the nearest other homestead. I assume that it is occupied either by a shepherd or by a forester. During heavy snowstorms the cottage may remain unapproachable for many days because these minor highways are left to await a thaw. One or two stone circles appear on the hillside near the cottage, set there as pounds for livestock. Most of the sheep are Cheviots (the word should be pronounced as 'Cheeviots'), a hardy breed, named after their native English hills, which have a small outcrop in Roxburghshire. During the eighteenth century a Northumbrian farmer crossed his Cheviot ewes with three Lincolnshire rams; twenty years later the flock had increased its yield of meat and fleece by thirty per cent. In 1792 Sir John Sinclair of Ulbster imported Cheviots into Caithness, where they became known as the Great Sheep. Other lairds soon discovered that an acre under Cheviots produced twice as much profit as did an acre under cattle, partly because three thousand sheep could be tended by only four shepherds. The Scottish Highlands never wholly recovered from this drastic innovation, which made thousands of families homeless, redundant, bitter. The Lowlands, however, were raising flocks long before an English breeder made the Cheviots famous. In 1550 Scotland produced six million pounds of wool, chiefly from Lowland sheep, but of a poor quality, most of it going to the Netherlands. In 1666 Galashiels founded its own Weaver's Corporation, and the railway ultimately enabled the town to serve as a junction for the Tweed Valley weaving centres at Hawick, Peebles, Selkirk and Langholm.

How well the Cheviot sheep merge with Liddesdale's lonely landscape. How handsome they are – the handsomest of all breeds; white-faced, sharp-withered, nimble as ballerinas. Eighty years ago they won more carcass prizes at Smithfield than did all the other breeds combined. What Elihu Burritt said of the Northumbrian Border a century ago is true of Liddesdale to-day: 'Sheep, of the Cheviot breed mostly, are nearly the sole inhabitants and industrials of this mountainous waste.' Burritt himself may have met various Borderers whose fathers had witnessed the Jacobite Rebellion in 1745. Without a doubt he became excited when he reached the frontier. 'This,' he exclaimed, 'is the Border-land! Here the fiercest antagonisms of hostile nationalities met in deadly conflict. Fire and blood, rapine and wrath blackened and reddened and ravaged for centuries across this bleak territory.' One of the Border ballads recounts the fate of Liddesdale raiders who invaded Northumberland:

> Now Liddesdale has ridden a raid,
> But I wat they had better hae staid at hame;
> For Michael o' Winfield he is dead,
> And Jock o' the Side is prisoner ta'en.

Another ballad tells of a Northumbrian, Hobie Noble, who was evidently ignoble:

> Now Hobie he was an English man,
> And born into Bewcastle dale;
> But his misdeeds they were sae great
> They banished him to Liddesdale.

Burritt, of course, found a kindlier scene: 'The sheep of the English and Scotch shepherds feed side by side on these mountainous heights, in spite of Stirling and Bannockburn, of Flodden and Falkirk.' The human population was still sparse, and scarcity of churches amazed Burritt when he approached Hawick: 'Calling at a station on the railway that passes through it, I was told by the master that the nearest church or chapel was sixteen miles in one direction, and over twenty in another. It is doubtful if so large a churchless space could be found in Iowa or even Kansas.' There are not many other parts of Britain where you can travel nearly twenty miles through scenery so wild as Liddesdale, so free from the noise and pollution which long ago led Gerard Manley Hopkins to complain that vast areas of our countryside were 'seared with trade . . . smeared, bleared'.

On, then, the lane goes, into solitude and silence and glimpses of distant sheep. Suddenly, away to the left, the site of Shankend Station appears, and beside it a signalbox; (nowadays an office for foresters); but the station has gone, and no trains cross the handsome viaduct overlooking an isolated farm. At this point on the journey a stranger may wonder whether the lane ever will reach Hawick. I well remember by own first journey and the surprise when at last I saw a small signpost which from a distance looked rather like the gibbet above Inkpen on the Berkshire Ridgeway. One finger of the signpost pointed north-east to Bonchester Bridge, along a lane that looked even lonelier than the Shankend route. If you do turn north-east, an hour and a half of walking will bring you to the road between Hawick and the Border at Carter Bar, formerly a scene of many skirmishes despite the fact that the Wardens from both kingdoms met there to settle disputes peaceably. One of the Border ballads describes a meeting in 1575, when Sir John Carmichael spoke for Scotland, and Sir John Forster for England; the subject being a Tyndale horse-thief named Robson. Harsh words were spoken, tempers were lost, swords were drawn. At the very moment when the English troop was forcing the Scots downhill, a party arrived from Jedburgh, whereupon the English withdrew, outnumbered and disarrayed. This so-called 'Fray of Redeswire' was said to be the last of the Border forays. Carter Bar to-day is a scenic trophy for both sides, proving that No Man's Land has become as placid as Wordsworth's battlefield,

> In stillness left when slaughter is no more . . .

Through that stillness the lane to Hawick bears westward, descending gradually from the high moor. Soon it rejoins the railway near Stobs Camp, another vanished station. A white farmhouse stands on the right, half-hidden among wind-breaking trees. More trees are seen, and presently a long wall, enclosing an estate. The lane becomes a road. The stream becomes a river. Cars are heard, and the outskirts of Hawick appear, creating a clash between hideous council houses (some of the doors are painted mauve) and handsome period houses beside the river. Finally, you reach the main street, crammed with traffic and people. Amid this loud scurry the cottage at Lime Kiln Edge seems a thousand miles away, alone in a land of wind, water, curlews, sheep. Robert Louis Stevenson remembered just such a scene, and wished that he could return there, if only in imagination:

> O to dream! to awake and wander
> There, and with delight to take and render
> Through the trance of silence,
> Quiet breath . . .

Whenever I reach Hawick, I, too, look back on the way I have come,

> for there, among the flowers and grasses
> Only the mightier movement sounds and passes;
> Only winds and rivers,
> Life and death.

A Green Road: Westmorland

Mile upon mile in the moonlight,
Fallow and ploughland and lea,
Mansion and cottage and castle,
Stretching away to the sea.

Strangers they lie, in the moonlight,
Many a mile from my hill,
Orchard and parkland and paddock,
Eloquent, silent, and still.

Strangers they lie, yet in friendship
They reach through the night for my hand,
Mountain and valley and forest,
The core and pith of our land . . .

Lanes that I know are entwining
Motionless into the breeze,
Scented with perfume of hawthorn,
Girded and guarded by trees;

Farms now asleep till the morning,
Mastiffs at peace with their chain,
Wombs of ineffable gladness
And immemorial pain;

Churches embowered among yew trees,
Transepts a thousand years old,
Gates all alone in the meadows,
Shepherds awake by their fold;

Centuries, centuries living,
Touched but not troubled by time,

Cradle of sailors and soldiers,
Mistress of masters of rhyme.

Brace me, you men of this England,
Who lived in these valleys and hills,
Who fashioned our manner of living,
Our barns and our bields and our mills.

Acknowledge me, though I am stranger,
From far distant hills in this land;
Grant me a blessing, my Mother;
Father, I reach for your hand.

Ichabod: Berkshire and Wiltshire

I walk where shovel, pick, and axe
Once gleamed in sunlight while they laid
Deep foundations and muddy tracks
Over the grass and through the glade,
Advancing westward day by day
This unfrequented waterway.

I walk where cottage housewives stared
To see and hear the navvying crowd
Who felled the fox's covert; bared
The amber stubble; drained the shroud
Of stagnant pond-scum; through the hill
Tunnelled a fairway dark and eerie;
Their shovels sharp, their curses shrill,
The faces brown, their muscles weary.

I walk among the hidden grooves
Where many feet and many hooves
Once ventured while the horses hauled
Laden barges whose crewmen called
A drowsy keeper at his lock
On summer noons, or when the clock
Chimed dusky teatime, and the snow
Muffled a woman's voice below,
Crooning her infant son asleep
Within his cradle snug and deep.

I walk where barefoot urchins trod;
Where farriers at their forges shod
Immense and shaggy Shires; where inns
Redeemed a multitude of sins
With waterside compassion; where

The bargemen set a midnight snare,
And, as the sun rose, took good care
That dawn should jug the stolen hare.

I walk where few folk ever go
Unless in leisure hours to steer
A chugging pleasure-craft, or row
A lonely dinghy past the weir.

I walk through woods that greenly twine
Beneath the overhanging boughs
While thrushes sing, and fishes shine,
And rabbits bask, and cattle browse
Beside the water. All is still,
All is derelict, all forlorn,
Mourning the merchandise once borne
From coast to coast, uphill, downdale,
Without an engine or a sail,
Rising and falling through the locks
. . . Brass beds, bronze tubes,tin plates, stone blocks,
Dried fish, old iron, new ore, fresh fruit,
Ploughshares and fly wheels, hemp and jute,
Manure, molasses, pit-props, coal,
Charting an inland Pole to Pole,
Private and public cargoes, all
Hoping to reach their port-of-call

Before the sunset's fiery glow
Sent them to join the Watch Below.
And always I must walk alone
Unless I choose the random hours
When bankside scythesmen whet their stone,
And Izaak Waltons test their powers
Of fishery, and lovers stroll
Secretive as a midday mole
Seeking the darkness. Few indeed
Now walk beside this watery way,

And fewer still disturb the weed
As did those barges in their day,
Strung out like slow Armadas sent
Well-found with peaceable intent.

Today modernity's new loads
Travel by rail or lethal roads.
The miles that feet and hooves once trod
Are now a lonely Ichabod.